HOW THEY BUILT
OUR NATIONAL MONUMENTS

Also by Paul C. Ditzel

FIRE ENGINES, FIREFIGHTERS
EMERGENCY, AMBULANCE
FIRE ALARM!: The Story of a Fire Department
FIREFIGHTING: A New Look in the Old Firehouse

HOW THEY BUILT OUR NATIONAL MONUMENTS

Paul C. Ditzel

The Bobbs-Merrill Company, Inc.
INDIANAPOLIS / NEW YORK

Chapters one through five were originally published in somewhat different form in *The American Legion Magazine.*

Copyright © 1976 by Paul C. Ditzel

All rights reserved, including the right of reproduction in whole or in part in any form
Published by the Bobbs-Merrill Company, Inc.
Indianapolis   New York

Designed by Ingrid Beckman
Manufactured in the United States of America

First printing

Library of Congress Cataloging in Publication Data

Ditzel, Paul C
  How they built our national monuments.

  Includes index.
  SUMMARY: Stories behind the construction of ten famous United States monuments, including the White House, Liberty Bell, Washington Monument, Golden Gate Bridge, the Mt. Rushmore faces, Statue of Liberty, Hoover Dam, the U.S. Capitol Building, Old Ironsides and the Gateway Arch.
  1. Monuments—United States—Juvenile literature. 2. Historic sites—United States—Juvenile literature. 3. Historic buildings—Washington, D.C.—Juvenile literature. 4. United States—Description and travel—1960- [1. Monuments. 2. Historic sites. 3. United States] I. Title.

E159.D624   973   76-11633
ISBN 0-672-52124-5

To Bob Pitkin and Jim Swartz,
who know how to build writers

PHOTO CREDITS:

U.S. Department of the Interior,
    National Park Service: pp. 17, 19, 31, 33, 37, 41, 43, 47, 49, 60, 65, 67, 89, 91, 94, 96, 98, 102, 105, 108, 110, 112, 114, 116, 118, 122, 123, 171, 175, 180, 183
Bethlehem Steel Corporation: pp. 146, 148, 151, 153, 156, 160, 162, 164, 165, 167
Official U.S. Navy Photos: pp. 70, 72, 75, 77, 83, 84, 86
Library of Congress: pp. 38, 56, 64, 92, 100
U.S. Department of the Interior,
    Bureau of Reclamation: pp. 126, 128, 130, 134, 139
Independence National Historical Park Collection: pp. 8, 9, 11, 14
Pittsburgh-Des Moines Steel Company: pp. 173, 178
City of Los Angeles, Department of Water and Power: pp. 137, 143
Hugh Miller, *Washington Post:* p. 29
Maryland Historical Society: p. 23
Courtesy Office of Public Buildings and Public Parks
    of the National Capital: p. 53
U.S. Department of Ships: p. 79

CONTENTS

		Acknowledgments	viii
		Introduction	1
I	/	The Liberty Bell	7
II	/	The White House	22
III	/	The Capitol Building	36
IV	/	Washington National Monument	51
V	/	Old Ironsides	69
VI	/	The Statue of Liberty	88
VII	/	The Faces on Mount Rushmore	104
VIII	/	Hoover Dam	125
IX	/	The Golden Gate Bridge	145
X	/	The Gateway Arch	170
		Bibliography	185
		Index	190

ACKNOWLEDGMENTS

THE AUTHOR gratefully acknowledges the help of the many people who encouraged him during the research and writing of this book:

Felix Ayres, Glendale, California, Public Library, who brought to my attention the fascinating story of how they built the Gateway Arch in St. Louis.

Fred Bell, Visual Information Specialist, National Park Service, U.S. Department of the Interior, and his staff, who showed me every courtesy while assisting in the collection of illustrative material.

The Bethlehem Steel Corporation. There were many officials of this firm who went far beyond what any author might expect to ensure that I lacked neither material nor photographs for the Golden Gate Bridge chapter. In each instance, they requested that any acknowledgment go to the Corporation, rather than to them individually.

Mrs. Joan Bartel and **Ms. Anita King,** Reference Librarians, Los Angeles City Library, for their many courtesies and suggestions during the preparation of this book.

Palmer Brown, Jr., Book Evaluation Unit, Los Angeles County Public Library, a longtime and true friend whose constant encouragement makes me appreciate all the more how far the professional library sciences have advanced.

Kenneth L. Black, Administrative Assistant to Barry M. Goldwater, Jr., 27th District Congressman of California. A devoted history buff, Ken helped to expedite my research in that rich lode of historical ore that is the nation's capital.

Milton B. Dollinger, Assistant Vice President, and **Mrs. Vera Leclercq** of the Chessie System, for the great amount of effort they spent in verifying material contained in the Washington National Monument chapter.

Steve Hinderer, Director of Public Affairs, City of Los Angeles Department of Water and Power; **Bill Kelly,** Assistant to the Director of Public Affairs; and **Lawrence Schneider,** Engineer-in-Charge of Design and Construction, City of Los Angeles Department of Water and Power, for their assistance with illustrations and material. I am especially grateful to Mr. Schneider for reading my Hoover Dam chapter and suggesting changes where necessary.

Mrs. Mary Krug, Deputy Director, Public Affairs, National Park Service, U.S. Department of the Interior, Washington, D.C., who was of great help in expediting research into various NPS-supervised parks and memorials.

Tyrone G. Martin, Commander, U.S. Navy, 53rd in Command of the *Constitution*, who gave freely of his time and expertise as a naval historian to read my chapter on *Old Ironsides* and to suggest changes.

Mrs. Adoreen McCormick, Legislative Liaison Officer, Library of Congress, Washington, D.C., for her many courtesies while I was researching in the Library of Congress.

Jerry Kearns, Reference Librarian, Library of Congress, Washington, D.C., for his excellent suggestions and kind assistance during the photographic and illustration phases of the book.

Warren A. McCullough, Public Affairs Specialist, Independence National Historical Park, Philadelphia, who extended many courtesies and was instrumental in providing me with illustrations of the Liberty Bell.

Mrs. Evelyn Myers, Photography Section, Bureau of Reclamation, U.S. Department of the Interior, whose enthusiasm for my project was such that she energetically provided much research data and other information on Hoover Dam.

Albert H. Redles, Retired Corporation Executive, Philadelphia, for his many years of close friendship, his constant encouragement, and his assistance in obtaining much information in the Philadelphia area.

Charles A. Ross, Acting Superintendent, Jefferson National Expansion Memorial, St. Louis, Missouri, for his keen interest and cooperation while the Gateway Arch chapter was in preparation.

John Stringer, Franklin Institute, Philadelphia, who generously made photographs of the Liberty Bell available to me.

Joseph Doan Thomas of the National Archives, Washington, D.C., whose deep historical knowledge and expertise in photo-selection was deeply appreciated.

Eugene Vance, Reference Librarian, California State University, Northridge, California, for his excellent cooperation in assisting me while retrieving historical information from this superb library, one of the newest and most complete in the United States, particularly in audio-visual materials.

Harvey D. Wickware, Superintendent, and **Arnold B. Simmons,** Chief Ranger, Mount Rushmore National Memorial, Keystone, South Dakota. If there was any way that they could have assisted me more while I was preparing this chapter, I cannot think of it. Their vigorous cooperation will forever be remembered by this author.

I would be deeply remiss if I did not make a special point of expressing my deep gratitude to my editor, **Walter Myers,** whose patience and enthusiastic encouragement from the start to the completion of this book will forever be appreciated. He has the editorial knack of knowing how to get that extra effort from his authors.

Introduction

GEORGE WASHINGTON, Thomas Jefferson, Abraham Lincoln, Harry Truman, Gerald Ford—and nearly every other President—shared a common interest. Like most of us, they were sidewalk-superintendents of construction. Washington had his own ideas about how the White House and the Capitol should be built. He frequently watched construction work and offered suggestions which, coming from the President, were tantamount to orders. On one occasion a suggestion of his was ignored. Washington told them to do it his way. And so they tore out all their own work and did. Jefferson also became incensed when the Capitol architect refused to follow his instructions to build a roof of glass instead of one of wood over the House of Representatives. Jefferson may not have been right, but he was President. And so the wood came out and the glass went in.

It might have seemed that the Civil War should take priority over the building of the Capitol dome, but Lincoln would not hear of postponing construction until the war was over. He ordered workers back on the job. "If people see the Capitol going on," said Lincoln, "it will be a sign to them that we intend the Union shall go on." The most dramatic—and most controversial—change in the appearance of the White House was made by Truman. To take advantage of evening breezes, he ordered workers to build a second-floor balcony. The Truman Balcony touched off a national furor among those who were opposed to changing the traditional look of the White House. But Truman built it anyway, and the United States Treasury had to print new twenty-dollar bills showing the change. President Ford avoided any such fuss when he decided to build a swimming pool. Ford eagerly watched construction proceed as the bill for the pool was paid by public donations.

Like the Presidents, the rest of us sidewalk-superintendents might have other ideas, but there is little likelihood that anybody would listen to them. We must content ourselves to watch while today's builders, with their fascinating derricks and other tools, go about the job of constructing tall buildings in downtown areas, high-rise apartments, and shopping malls covering entire city blocks in suburbs.

One day while sidewalk-superintending, I began to wonder how they built our famous structures, memorials and ships that are so familiar to us and, in many cases, cherished as national treasures. With the aid of friends and colleagues, including librarians, schoolteachers, historians, construction engineers, and my editors, I came up with a long list of excellent candidates. The list had to be shortened to ten because of book-length restrictions. Ultimately, the final choice had to be mine, and my selections were somewhat arbitrary, but in every case the choice came about because research unraveled fascinating stories-within-stories of how they built the chosen ten.

Although each chapter stands as a self-contained unit—just like the structures themselves—I found a number of common threads from the building of the Liberty Bell to the construction of the Gateway Arch. Common to all of them was the inspirational realization of what monumental works mankind is capable of accomplishing when there is a determination to do them. How audacious were those two young Philadelphia foundrymen, John Pass and John Stow, Jr., who had never cast a public bell in their lives. When the townspeople broke the first bell that came from England, Pass and Stow took sledgehammers to it and said they could melt it up, add some more metal, and make a better bell than that which had come from the foremost maker of bells in England, if not the world. Their first try was a failure. Despite public ridicule, they tried again, and finally produced the bell that one day would ring for freedom—the Liberty Bell.

And what about Gutzon Borglum? He was going on sixty years old and was not in the prime of life when he determined to overcome all sorts of obstacles in the forbidding wilderness of the Black Hills of South Dakota to create the four faces on Mount Rushmore, including the famous life-like glint in Lincoln's eyes. Or consider the determination of Joseph Strauss, who gambled his reputation as the foremost bridge-builder in the world when he took on the challenge of spanning one of the most treacherous bodies of navigable water in the world—the Golden Gate. The determination of Strauss and the builders of the Golden Gate Bridge never faltered, despite setback upon setback.

Determination, too, was the mark of those who built Hoover Dam. The Colorado River was one of the most dangerous rivers in the world. Man had been trying to tame the river during the four centuries since it had been discovered. Every attempt had failed. To build the Hoover Dam project was one of the most challenging architectural, engineering and construction jobs ever attempted by mankind. Then the United States Bureau of Reclamation and an outfit with as unlikely a name as Six Companies, Inc., tackled the job with an armada of equipment and an army of workers who built night and day until they finished the job that many had said was impossible. And they completed it more than two years ahead of schedule.

Another common bond among these structures is how close they came to never being built and, after they were, how even closer some came to destruction. During the American Revolution, the Liberty Bell was lugged away from Philadelphia and buried, else it undoubtedly would have been melted into bullets. After the bell was returned to Independence Hall, neighbors complained of its noise pollution (it was rung for everything from fire alarms to patriotic celebrations). Get rid of it, they said. The aging bell was sold for junk, but the scrap dealer who bought it changed his mind and said there was not enough salvageable metal in it to make it worth his while.

Congress was not certain that it wanted the President to have his own home, feeling that it might smack of a king's palace. Some said that a rented house was good enough for the President. When Congress decided to proceed with the house, the legislators made certain it would not rival the Capitol Building in size or majesty. Construction was often slipshod as well. The White House, changed by almost every President who thought he knew more about construction than the builders and rebuilders, became a firetrap. On Christmas Eve, 1929, while President Herbert Hoover was entertaining holiday guests, a fire caused severe damage to the West Wing and the Oval Office.

Every schoolboy knows the story of how Oliver Wendell Holmes's famous poem saved *Old Ironsides* from being scrapped. Not so well known is the fact that *Old Ironsides* was later scheduled to be towed to sea and blown to bits while being used as a target for warships on maneuvers. *Old Ironsides* was rebuilt again and again following public protests against scrapping it and massive appeals for public funds to restore it. Not the least of the contributions came from school students who donated their pennies to save her, just as they did in 1848, when it appeared the Washington National Monument would be abandoned. National "Give-a-Penny" campaigns in schools helped to raise money to get construction started again. Students did the same for the Statue of Liberty and were among the first to donate to the fund to create the faces on Mount Rushmore. Student contributions also helped to pay for President Ford's swimming pool.

Still another common thread woven throughout this book is the unusually long periods of time it took to build our national memorials. Political intrigue, jealousies, constant haggling over money to continue construction, and roadblocks of every imaginable sort became part of the story of their construction. Even then, work was done in bits and pieces. When the Washington National Monument was partly built, the New York *Tribune* said that "the big furnace chimney on the Potomac" should be abandoned. From start to finish, the construction of the Washington Monument took one century—spanning the terms of twenty-one Presidents. It took twenty-one years before the Statue of Liberty stood with her hand holding high the light of freedom at the entrance to New York Harbor. The delay was not the doing of her builder, Frédéric-Auguste Bartholdi, who loved America as much as he did his native France. The delay was due to an apathetic American public and Federal government. *The New York Times,* moreover, said the city did not need any lady in robes standing at the entrance to the city. That we ever got around to building the massive pedestal on which the Statue of Liberty stands was mostly due to the haranguing of newspaper publisher Joseph Pulitzer, who shamed Americans into building the pedestal. The Gateway Arch, as elegant a monument as could possibly stand to the memory of those who opened the westward expansion of the United States, may look simple, but it took forty-three years to build from concept to conclusion.

And how precise these builders were. When Borglum discovered an imperfection in the granite where the face of Jefferson was to be created, he changed his plans and tilted the face away from the crevice. Why bother? he was asked. Nobody would be able to see the imperfection from the ground, and it would be centuries before the elements eroded the granite enough to mar Jefferson's face. Replied Borglum, the consummate craftsman: "I have no intention of leaving a head on that mountain that in the course of five hundred or five thousand years will be without a nose." Impressive, too, was the precision work of the builders of the Golden Gate Bridge. Before they started to erect the famous twin towers, the concrete piers on which they were to stand were ground to a flat tolerance of one thirty-second inch to make certain the towers would stand straight and true. When they started to build the Gateway Arch, they knew they had a margin of error of only one sixty-fourth inch if the legs of the arch were to join in the middle. They solved the problem by taking instrument readings at night while focusing on lights at the tips of the arches when the temperatures along the stainless steel legs cooled to a uniform degree.

And what about the tools they used? When they built the White House starting in 1792, slaves scooped out the clay foundations. They mixed their own mortar, built brick kilns, cut timbers in surrounding forest lands and hauled them to the construction site. There were no skilled workers in America and very little industry to supply construction materials, so architect James Hoban had to send to Europe for stonecutters, carpenters and bricklayers. Prior to the start of work on the Hoover Dam Project in 1931, a railroad was built from near Las Vegas to the site of the dam. During the construction, cement mixers were producing more than sixteen tons a minute; by the time the dam was completed, the railroad had brought in five million barrels of cement, eighteen million pounds of structural steel, twenty-one million pounds of watergates and valves, and 840 miles of pipe.

From the time they started to build the Liberty Bell in 1751 until they finished the Gateway Arch more than two hundred years later, fascinating advances were made in construction techniques, and particularly in the tools that were used. How would the skilled carpenters who carved the mighty oak framework for the hull of *Old Ironsides* and put it together with Paul Revere's copper nails have reacted had they been able to see how the men who built the Gateway Arch used gamma-radiation cameras and computers?

The dangers multiplied over the years as American construction workers took on greater challenges. It is both curious and a testimonial to the builders' stress on safety that so few lives were lost. But there were lapses. Capitol architect John Lenthal frequently warned of the dangers of the poor construction work that was being forced on him. He expressed concern over the possibility of falling arches, and that is exactly what happened: Lenthal himself was crushed under one that collapsed.

It is incredible that nobody was killed at Mount Rushmore, despite the fact that Borglum and his workers were continually using dynamite and hanging over the side of the mountain in suspension chairs while chipping away at the rock. There were some narrow escapes: a lightning storm in the forest set off dynamite that did little more harm than to blow the shoes off a worker. Not long after, a cable car loaded with workers ran away, but none were killed. At the time the Golden Gate Bridge was being built, it was an engineering rule of thumb that one worker would be killed for every $1 million it cost to build a bridge. Unprecedented safety features helped to save many lives, including those of nineteen workers who fell into a safety net. They formed a social organization and called it The Half Way To Hell Club. Eleven others were not so lucky, but these eleven deaths were far fewer than had been anticipated.

Certainly one of the most dangerous construction jobs ever undertaken was the Gateway Arch. There it was estimated that thirteen workers would be killed—but not one was. The little-known story of how they did it while working more than six hundred feet in the sky on platforms that constantly swayed in the stiff winds during the summer and winter has never been completely told. One of the builders of the Gateway Arch agreed to tell me how it was done and how the Arch was completed despite a last-minute emergency which threatened the entire project. His only request: "Don't mention my name. Some of the other hardhats would think I was bragging."

It will occur to readers that the builders of the ten monuments and structures described in this book were entitled to boast at least a little bit. These milestones in the construction history of America will forever be treasured, and their pricelessness will grow with each passing year. It is hoped that this book will serve as a reminder of the determination, skill and ingenuity of those largely forgotten men who built them.

The Liberty Bell

SOMEHOW THE LIBERTY BELL survived its ugly-duckling childhood to joyously ring out the celebration of the July 1776 signing of the Declaration of Independence in Philadelphia's State House. Fresh out of the casting mold, the bell broke the first time it was clanged. A second attempt brought forth a bell that sounded like a frog croaking instead of a bell clanging. The bell and the two foundrymen who made it became the laughingstock of Philadelphia. They tried again, and finally came up with the bell we know today.

The Liberty Bell was never healthy. It cracked at least twice. A metal expert diagnosed the Liberty Bell's illness as a malignancy of the molecules. The bell was said to be suffering from distemper. Another metallurgist said the bell had the wobbles. There were scores of ideas for fixing the crack. Nobody ever did close it, because, as Independence Hall Superintendent Melford O. Anderson said, "The crack must remain forever as a symbol of freedom in the United States."

Ill health was not the worst of the bell's problems. Many said the sound of the bell was noise pollution of the foulest sort. The bell barely escaped being melted into bullets and cannonballs. Later, when nobody wanted the old bell, it was put up for auction, but before that happened it was sold to a junkman who later changed his mind and said it was not worth hauling away. Traveling around the United States, the bell came back to Philadelphia in worse shape than when it left. Still later, radicals plotted to blow the bell to pieces.

Pouring the Liberty Bell.

Since it was unwanted and unloved for so many years, how did it happen that a $139.66 bell that came from the casting pot of two men who were not in the business of making bells today occupies an $800,000 home especially built for it during the celebration of America's Bicentennial? Therein lies the story of how they built, rebuilt, and patched together the Liberty Bell.

The story begins a quarter of a century before the signing of the Declaration of Independence. In 1751 a wooden tower was being added to the State House where Pennsylvania assemblymen met. That house would become known as Independence Hall. On October 16 the Quaker assemblymen decided there were two reasons for buying a bell for the tower. First, the bell they had was too small to be heard throughout Philadelphia when it called assemblymen to meetings, called courts into session, and notified townspeople to gather to hear official proclamations. Second, the bell would honor the fiftieth anniversary of religious freedom in the province.

There was no bell in America as big as the one the assemblymen wanted. It would have to come from England. The legislators left the size, weight, and inscription to the discretion of Assembly Speaker Isaac Norris and his associates, Thomas Leech and Edward Warner. Norris was a wealthy Quaker with a profound knowledge of the

Bible. He chose an inscription adapted from Leviticus 25:10, the third book of the Old Testament. God, speaking to Moses on Mount Sinai, says the Israelites must celebrate their liberation from Egypt by holding a jubilee every fifty years: "And ye shall hallow the fiftieth year, and proclaim liberty throughout *all* the land unto all the inhabitants thereof: it shall be a jubile unto you; and ye shall return every man unto his possession; and ye shall return every man unto his family."

Norris knew that the circumference at the top of the bell would be too small for the entire text. For the inscription he chose eleven words of the verse which he ordered to be "well shaped" in large letters: "PROCLAIM LIBERTY THROUGHOUT ALL THE LAND UNTO ALL THE INHABITANTS THEREOF. Lev. XXV. 10." To this day, many people believe the inscription refers to the Declaration of Independence rather than to religious freedom in Pennsylvania.

Instructions to "get us a good bell of about 2000 pounds" were sent to Robert Charles, Pennsylvania's agent in London. "Let the bell be cast by the best workmen and examined carefully before it is shipped." The urgency of the request was impressed on Charles. He was told it would be easier to hang the bell within the next few months while the scaffolding remained around the tower. Charles quickly hired the foremost English manufacturer of church bells, Thomas Lester's Whitechapel Foundry of London.

First journey of the Liberty Bell as it leaves Philadelphia to escape being melted into bullets and cannonballs by British troops.

The bell arrived in Philadelphia late in the summer of 1752. Eager to try it out, the assemblymen ordered the bell set up in the State House yard. Townspeople gathered to hear its first ringing clang. The bell had but one clang in it. With a single stroke of the clapper, the bell cracked. The assemblymen were dismayed. The bell could not immediately be returned to London because there were no ships leaving with space to carry it. It might be a year before another bell could be obtained. By then the tower would be done and the scaffolding taken down. Nor was there any guarantee the Whitechapel Foundry could do better. Norris was, moreover, unhappy with the sound of the fatal clang, which he described as "too high and brittle."

A solution was suggested by two young foundrymen, John Pass and John Stow, Jr. They had never cast a bell, they said, but they would attempt it by using the metal from the shattered one. Although the Pass and Stow foundry was pathetically crude compared with the one at Whitechapel, the assemblymen decided to give them a chance. Pass and Stow sledgehammered the bell into chunks small enough to fit into their melting pots. Before casting the new bell they melted a few pieces, mixed in some other metals, and made several small bells which they tested for sound and strength. Their experiments suggested a sturdier bell could be cast by adding an ounce and a half of copper to each pound of the Whitechapel metal.

At last all was ready. Pass and Stow, their shirtsleeves rolled up and long leather aprons covering their red knee breeches, tended the molten metal bubbling in the cauldrons. They perspired profusely by the glare of the blazing furnace, as did Norris and several assemblymen who came to watch. Pass and Stow ladled the metal. It "ran well" into the "masterful mould," said Norris, who judged the quality of the inscription to be better than the original. When the bell cooled, it was hauled to the State House yard, where a huge crowd gathered for a celebration.

The bell was slowly hoisted by ropes and pulleys while workmen on the tower scaffolding steadied it. They swung the hulking thing into place in the steeple and secured the bell to a wooden yoke. The bell was rung. The crowd cheered, the festivities started, and the experts began a somber debate over the bell's sound qualities. Instead of the loud clanging tones which had been expected, the Pass and Stow bell went *clong*. A critic said the bell sounded like a frog croak-

Liberty Bell loaded on flatcar prior to leaving for Chicago visit.

ing. Another said the noise resembled that of two coal shovels being banged together. The odd tone probably resulted from the addition of the extra copper. Pass and Stow were embarrassed by the ruckus, the more so, declared Norris, because "they were so tiezed with the witticisms of the town."

To redeem themselves, Pass and Stow vowed to try again. If they failed, the bell would go back to England. Everyone expected Pass and Stow to fail, and perhaps Norris did as well. In their second mixture, the foundrymen probably added a quantity of tin to restore the tone destroyed by the excess copper. Otherwise, their second bell nearly duplicated the first. It stood five feet three inches and weighed 2,080 pounds. The bell was twelve feet in circumference around the bottom lip, seven and a half feet around the crown, and two feet three inches over the crown. The bell was thickest, three inches, near the lip and tapered to one and a quarter inches toward the crown. Six loops for rigid attachment to a yoke were cast into the top of the bell. The clapper was thirty-eight inches long. Into its bottom knob was cast a hand grip for striking the clapper against the sides. The "PROCLAIM LIBERTY" inscription encircled the crown. Underneath it were these additional words: "By order of the Assembly of the Province of Pensylvania for the State House in Philada. Pass and Stow. Philada. MDCCLIII."

Hauled to the State House, the bell was hoisted to the tower and mounted on a long thick crossbeam. Although the bell's tone drew some criticism, everyone agreed that it was acceptable. There is no record that a second celebration was even discussed. Philadelphians apparently were satisfied to let well enough alone after waiting nearly two years for their bell. They paid scant attention to the fact that Pass and Stow, in their zeal to cast a bell which would ring out loud and clear, made one error. Their misspelling of Pennsylvania remains to this day for all the world to see.

Philadelphians were unhappy with English rule when the bell officially tolled for the first time, August 27, 1753, to call a meeting of assemblymen. They voted to ignore an order from the British Lord Justices of the Crown to discontinue issuing money. The bell was used for many purposes, including calls to worship by members of St. Paul's and sounding fire alarms. The town apparently was so delighted with the bell that little excuse was needed to set the bell to bonging. Philadelphians who lived nearby complained of the racket. They said that the noise could make ill people sicker, that the bell's "uncommon size and unusual sound extremely dangerous and may prove fatal." They asked assemblymen to forbid the bell from being rung except on public occasions. The request was ignored, but assemblymen did vote to strengthen the tower. They feared that vibrations from the frequent ringing might cause the steeple to collapse.

The bell rang out milestones in the deepening crisis with Great Britain. Its clapper was muffled, probably with rags or rope, on October 31, 1765, when the bell tolled a dirge as the Stamp Act taxes became law. Three years later the bell called merchants to the State House to protest England's Parliamentary Acts prohibiting the manufacture of hats, woolen goods, and iron and steel. After the Boston Tea Party, the bell called citizens to hear resolutions denouncing buyers and sellers of tea. Following the Battle of Lexington, the bell rang once again. A crowd of eight thousand cheered its approval of a resolution "to associate, for the purpose of defending with arms, their lives, liberty and property against all attempts to deprive them of them."

The State House bell summoned delegates to meetings of the Continental Congress during debate preceding the adoption of the Declaration of Independence, July 4, 1776. The bell did not, however, peal that memorable Thursday when the Declaration was ratified. It was decided to wait until four days later, noon, Monday, July 8, to make the official proclamation. The extra time was needed to publish and distribute copies of the Declaration to the colonies and Commander-in-Chief George Washington of the Army, and to prepare for what was expected to be a massive public celebration.

July 8 dawned bright and clear. The sun promised a hot day. By noon the heat had kept most of Philadelphia's thirty-five thousand people home, and only a few thousand had gathered in front of the State House. Colonel John Nixon stood on a platform and read the Declaration of Independence: "We hold these truths to be self-evident, that all men are created equal, that they are endowed by their Creator with certain unalienable Rights, that among these are Life, Liberty and the pursuit of Happiness. . . ." Afterward, as the crowd cheered, Assembly doorkeeper Andrew McNair set the bell to pealing. All church bells joined in. The bells "rang out all day and almost all night," said John Adams, who was to become our second President. Many years afterward somebody started the story that the Liberty Bell's famous crack resulted from McNair's overly enthusiastic ringing. But it was not until exactly fifty-nine years later, to the day, that the bell would crack.

No one is sure when the bell became known as the Liberty Bell. The bell had many names, including the Province Bell, the Bell of the Revolution, and the Independence Bell. Many historians say the Liberty Bell name originated shortly after 1839, some sixty-three years after the Declaration of Independence, when an anonymous author published an antislavery pamphlet, "The Liberty Bell."

During the War of Independence, the Liberty Bell was endangered when British General William Howe led an army of occupation toward Philadelphia. Congress ordered the immediate removal of all bells to Northampton (later Allentown, Pennsylvania), a munitions-making center for the Continental Army. Neither patriotism nor sentiment dictated the action. The British were certain to melt the Liberty Bell and the others into bullets and cannonballs. If the bells had

GRAHAM'S MAGAZINE.

Vol. XLIV.   PHILADELPHIA, JUNE, 1854.   No. 6.

Ringing out the Declaration of Independence.

to be recast, it would be better to put them into American muskets and cannon.

The Liberty Bell and ten other bells were loaded onto carts as part of a seven-hundred-wagon train of refugees fleeing Philadelphia. The bell bulked large on the wagon of John Jacob Mickley, who regularly hauled brandy to Philadelphia. The weight of the bell caused Mickley's wagon to collapse in front of the Moravian Brethren House in Bethlehem, Pennsylvania. The Liberty Bell was manhandled onto another wagon, which took it to Northampton's Zion Reformed Church. Auditorium floorboards were pried up, and a hole was dug. The Liberty Bell was lowered by ropes into the hole, and the flooring was replaced. The Liberty Bell remained in this vault for about a year. It was returned to the State House, and later, in October 1781, pealed the news of General Charles Cornwallis's surrender to Washington at Yorktown.

In subsequent years the Liberty Bell rang good news and bad. It tolled a welcome to President Washington when he came to Philadelphia, and its muffled clapper tolled his death in 1799. For ten years it called United States Congressmen to the State House, and it celebrated each Fourth of July as it similarly rang out on New Year's Eve. The Liberty Bell triumphantly pealed the victory of the *Constitution (Old Ironsides)* over the British frigate *Guerrière* during the War of 1812. The muffled bell also tolled a dirge as, one by one, the signers of the Declaration of Independence died.

In 1816 Pennsylvania Commonwealth legislators voted to abandon the decaying State House and to move to a new capitol building in Harrisburg. To pay for construction, they decided to sell the State House and the Liberty Bell. An appraisal showed the property might be auctioned to real estate developers for $150,000. An alternative plan was suggested: Sell the Liberty Bell and the State House property for $70,000 to Philadelphia, which could do whatever it chose with the building and bell. Before public auction became necessary, Philadelphia bought the property, and the Liberty Bell with it.

Saved from what would soon become a worse peril, the Liberty Bell rang out the fiftieth anniversary of the Declaration of Independence. Four days later, July 8, 1826, the bell tolled the deaths of two former Presidents: Thomas Jefferson, who wrote the Declaration of Independence, and John Adams, who assisted him. In 1828 Philadelphia hired John Wilbank, a foundryman, to cast a new bell with a new steeple clock. This bell was to replace the Liberty Bell and be twice its size. As part payment, Wilbank agreed to take down the Liberty Bell, which was estimated to have a junk value of four hundred dollars.

Wilbank had second thoughts about the bargain when he started to remove the bell from the tower. He found that the cost of lowering and hauling it away would be higher than he had expected. Illustrating the value then placed on the Liberty Bell, Wilbank is said to have complained, "Drayage costs are more than the bell is worth." He left the bell hanging, and Philadelphia immediately sued for breach of contract. A compromise was reached. Wilbank agreed to pay court costs, and Philadelphia kept the bell.

On July 8, 1835, the Liberty Bell's muffled clapper tolled during the funeral parade for one of America's greatest Chief Justices of the United States, John Marshall, whose monumental work had strengthened the Constitution. Sometime during those hours, the eighty-two-year-old bell cracked. The fracture was about as wide as your little finger and extended from the lip upward to about two-thirds of the way to the crown.

Metallurgists later explained why the bell had cracked. "The Liberty Bell is suffering from an organic disease of long standing," said Wilfred Jordan of Philadelphia, who in 1916 came up with his theory of the malignancy of the molecules.

"As with many people," he continued, "a disorder might be called hereditary and date from birth, so the defects of this old relic date from its first casting in England.

"This organic trouble arises from the scientific truth that all metal castings are subject to internal stresses due to natural shrinkage in cooling. These are known as 'cooling strains,' and the . . . fracture in the Liberty Bell was most probably due to such a cause. . . . Each time the heavy clapper struck the bell, the molecules contiguous to the flaw were thrown into violent vibration and what is known to metallurgists as 'breaking down in detail' took place. . . . In plain words, the crack extended at first perhaps only a millionth of an inch. . . . Such a minute flaw may [have taken] . . . years to reach the surface, even under the vibrations caused by the strokes of a bell clapper . . . "

Another metallurgist, Alexander E. Outerbridge, Jr., of the Franklin Institute, Philadelphia, who was to play a significant role in doctoring the Liberty Bell, said, "It is no hyperbolical figure of

View of the Liberty Bell through Independence Hall corridor.

speech to say that the venerated Liberty Bell is afflicted with a serious disease. Metallurgists have adopted into their technical jargon the term 'diseases of metals,' and recognize several with maladies. I have no hesitation in saying that the bell has . . . distemper."

Outerbridge noted the brittleness of the original bell, as well as the Pass and Stow addition of copper to strengthen the mixture and their probable subsequent use of tin to restore the tone. He drew the conclusion that, "under the circumstances, the casting cannot possibly have been of a homogeneous composition, and the bell was, therefore, subject to abnormal shrinkage and cooling strains." Outerbridge added that tests made in remelting pure copper several times showed that each melting caused it to lose strength and resilience.

Most people believe the bell was forever silenced when it cracked. Not so. It rang, but not very well, in 1846 to celebrate Washington's Birthday. To protect the bell from further damage by vibration, the edges of the fracture were filed, thus widening the crack to about three-quarters of an inch. The scratch marks can still be seen. The metal filings were cast into a miniature Liberty Bell, which is in the Independence Hall museum. Seven years later the Liberty Bell was taken down from the tower and put on public display.

There have been many proposals for repairing the bell so that it can ring again. In 1959 Albert A. Hughes of Mears & Stainback Foundry, successors to the old Whitechapel Foundry, offered to fix the Liberty Bell free as a gesture of British gratitude for America's role in World War II. Like all such offers, the proposal was declined.

Since the Liberty Bell was broken, it might be expected that it could no longer elude the melting pot. But the crack seemed to have had the opposite effect. It brought the Liberty Bell national fame and esteem it had never before enjoyed. By 1876, when America celebrated its hundredth birthday with a gigantic Centennial Exposition in Philadelphia, the bell was visited by many people. It was in too bad shape to be moved to the Exposition grounds. Even if it had been moved, the Liberty Bell might have been upstaged by the display of the forearm and torch of the still unfinished Statue of Liberty.

In 1885 the Liberty Bell left Independence Hall for the second time when it was taken by railroad flatcar to New Orleans for the Cotton States Industrial Exposition. During the next thirty-three years the bell visited Chicago, Atlanta, Charleston, St. Louis, and

The Liberty Bell in Independence Hall.

Boston, where it was displayed as part of a patriotic celebration at Bunker Hill. Returning from Chicago, it stopped in Allentown. Everyone in America, it seemed, wanted to see the bell. As invitations flooded in, a group of Philadelphians, including descendants of some signers of the Declaration of Independence, sued to halt the trips for fear of causing further damage to the bell. At first rebuffed, their pleas were heeded when a new crack was discovered in 1907. The zigzag fracture was a continuation of the original crack and extended to the right, up and around the crown, for nearly a quarter of its circumference.

Outerbridge, one of those who had argued that the bell was too sick to travel, was hired to minister to it. He found that the strain of the fracture was gradually pulling the bell apart. The metallurgist recommended that four padded stilts be placed under the lip of the bell to relieve this pressure. Later, Outerbridge recommended four more stilts. He designed a spiderlike device of inch-thick wrought-iron straps. The legs of the spider came from a hub inside the bell and were mounted on the clapper support. The spider legs ended in six equally spaced claws which were clamped to the edge of the lip to hold the bell together. Constant tension was provided by adjustable screws. About this time the upper and lower ends of the first fracture were secured by bolts to further prevent the Liberty Bell from falling apart.

Outerbridge soon noted that he had doctored the bell all too well. San Franciscans invited the bell to their city in 1915 during the Panama-Pacific International Exposition. Philadelphians debated the wisdom of the trip. Outerbridge warned against it. But a plea signed by 200,000 California students could not be denied. The Liberty Bell made the trip and returned safely. The journey was the bell's longest—and last—outside Philadelphia.

The infirmities of age were once more showing by the early 1960s, when the Franklin Institute was again called to tend the ailments of the Liberty Bell. A study showed the crack had not spread, but the bronze pedestal on which the bell stood was bent. The Liberty Bell, said Franklin's technicians, was suffering from the wobbles.

A new steel pedestal was called for, plus new vertical supports to provide greater rigidity. This treatment would cure the wobbles. Although the original yoke had been reinforced with a steel plate in 1929, better support was needed. Temperature and humidity changes required constant tightening of the jumbo bolts in the wood beam. The bolts were replaced with better-gripping ones. A T-shaped steel support was inconspicuously mounted in the yoke, which was first taken to the Franklin Institute for the delicate insertion.

The Liberty Bell remained in Independence Hall and was lowered onto a doughnut-shaped trough of concrete to absorb the weight and to make sure that the crack did not widen. The job took two months. In the spring of 1962 the bell was mated once more with its yoke.

For the next thirteen years the Liberty Bell stood in a ground-floor vestibule of Independence Hall. Neither panes of glass nor iron bars separated the Liberty Bell from the nearly two million visitors who annually stand in hushed reverence before this priceless national treasure. Men remove their hats in silent tribute while visitors reach out and run their hands across the rugged surface and touch the famous crack. In 1965 three members of a radical organization were arrested before they could carry out a plot to dynamite the Liberty Bell, the Washington Monument, and the Statue of Liberty.

In celebration of the United States Bicentennial in 1976, the Liberty Bell was given a home of its own about a block north of Independence Hall. The popularity of the bell had by then made it necessary to find more space for visitors. Special precautions make it virtually impossible for anybody to harm the bell. Visitors can see the Liberty Bell and, behind it, Independence Hall and the clock tower where the bell once hung. They can touch the bell during the day, and they can look through large windows at the dramatically floodlighted bell at night. By pushing a button, they will hear a recorded story of the bell that some two hundred years ago rang out the message, loud and clear for all the world to hear: "Proclaim liberty throughout all the land unto all the inhabitants thereof."

11

The White House

SINCE IT WAS FIRST BUILT, the White House has been rebuilt three times and remodeled and redecorated so many times that nobody has been able to keep count. Every President has made changes. Harry Truman built a balcony. Calvin Coolidge added a sewing room for his wife. Franklin D. Roosevelt put in an indoor swimming pool. Richard Nixon covered it over and made a larger press room. Gerald Ford built an outdoor pool with public donations, including twenty-one cents from students of a Los Angeles school.

Presidents' wives have had their say, too. No other First Lady did more than Jacqueline Kennedy, who redecorated the White House and turned it into an exquisite gallery of historical art and antique furnishings. Mrs. Kennedy hung early nineteenth-century blue wallpaper in the family dining room. Betty Ford said the paper was "kind of depressing." She had it removed and stored in the Smithsonian Institution in case some future President's wife wanted it. Then she had the room painted bright yellow.

Even before the White House was built, it was fair game for anybody with a pet idea of how it should look. President George Washington was living in a rented house in Philadelphia, at that time the nation's capital, when a national contest was announced in 1792 for the best design of the planned President's House and the Capitol Building. Judges included Washington, Thomas Jefferson and three District of Columbia commissioners. The winner would get his choice of five hundred dollars or a gold medal.

Among the entries was a grotesque drawing of a house with statues around the outside walls and gladiators locked in battle over the front door. Another came from an anonymous architect who signed his entry "A.Z." This design suggested a palace with an ornate dome in the center and marble columns on all sides. "A.Z." was later discovered to be none other than one of the judges, Thomas Jefferson.

Soon after the contest started, James Hoban, a thirty-year-old architect from Charleston, South Carolina, met the President. Washington said Georgian-style architecture, like that of his home at Mount Vernon, appealed to him most. Not only that, said the President, but the design must be simple to satisfy Congress. Some Congressmen feared that a magnificent executive mansion would smack

Design for the President's House, submitted by James Diamond of Maryland.

of a king's palace. There were other Congressmen who said the President did not need a house. They suggested that a rented home was good enough and would save money, too. Most of all, Congressmen did not want a presidential mansion that would dwarf their planned Capitol Building.

With this inside information on what would most appeal to the judges, Hoban won first prize by sketching a simple, rectangular, box-shaped three-story mansion, 168 feet long, 85½ feet wide and 60 feet high. Porticoes, or porches, with four marble columns highlighted the north and south entrances. Six chimneys jutted from the gently tapering roof.

The mansion resembled that of the Duke of Leinster in Hoban's native Ireland. Historians say the design was cribbed from the typical Georgian-style house shown in James Gibbs's *Book of Architecture*, a popular builders' guide. The only major variations were three oval-shaped rooms, one over the other, located in the center of the house.

Still fearful of congressional criticism and aware that money would be short, Washington told Hoban to scratch the third-floor living quarters to save some of the estimated $400,000 building cost. The President and his family would make do on the second floor. Hoban was hired at $262 a year to supervise construction. The site was almost exactly in the geographical center of the ten-mile-square city master-planned by Pierre Charles L'Enfant. Land for the Federal city was donated by Virginia and Maryland, which also appropriated some construction funds. More money was to be raised by selling building lots in the city.

The cornerstone was laid in October 1792, with completion targeted for eight years later, when the Capitol Building would be completed and Congress would move to Washington. Hoban rented slaves from nearby plantations. By the following summer, foundations had been scooped out of the clay. Brick kilns were built. The slaves cut timbers from surrounding forests. Without skilled labor in this virtual wilderness, Hoban sent to Europe for stonecutters, carpenters, and bricklayers.

There were no buildings to house the work force. A shantytown of shacks, sheds, and outhouses was slapped together among the kilns, mortar-mixing puddles, stacks of pine boards and construction gear. Working conditions were less than ideal. Summer heat, high humidity, and mosquitoes were only a bit less bothersome than spring rains which turned building-supply roads into muddy quagmires that bogged oxcarts of supplies from Baltimore, Maryland, and Richmond, Virginia. In the summer, farmers forced supply carts to detour around their cornfields. Hoban, his thick Irish brogue keyed up with rage, ordered them to clear a path across their fields or he would ask Washington for troops to do it for them.

Gray sandstone for the exterior walls was hacked by slaves in Virginia's Aquia quarries and barged in via the Potomac River. Using block-and-tackle devices, the slaves lifted the stones into place. Ground-floor planking was laid on the bare ground, and the first- and second-floor pine framing was pounded together with hand-forged spikes. Slowly the President's House took shape. Washington occasionally came down from Philadelphia to sidewalk-superintend.

Fund-raising turned out to be more of a dream than reality. Lot sales were disappointing, and construction money ran low. Hoban cut more corners. He canceled the order for fire-resistant marble chimney blocks and built them of cheaper wood. Construction of the slate roof was postponed. Exposed to rain and snow, interior woodwork would rot by the time the President moved in. Despite Hoban's penny-pinching, he had to tell Washington that payrolls were not being met on time.

What effect, if any, all this had on Washington's attitude toward the Presidency is not known. In any event, he decided against a third term and retired to Mount Vernon, where he died before the house was finished. As the completion date neared, the building still was not done, but it was in good enough shape for President and Mrs. John Adams to move in. Or so Hoban told them. He ordered the craftsmen to tear down their shacks and outhouses and to make the area attractive for the arrival of the presidential family. The workers replied, "If shantytown goes, so will we." They said they had no place else to sleep, unless Hoban wanted them to move in with the President. Faced with a certain strike, Hoban backed down.

President Adams and his wife, Abigail, moved in on November 1, 1800. Only six rooms were partly finished, and the first-floor East Room not at all. This room, which one day would be used for official receptions of world leaders, nationally televised press conferences, poetry readings, ballet and rock music festivals, was used by Mrs. Adams to do the family laundry. She was as unhappy as a First Lady could be. And with good cause.

The house was cold, drafty, and barnlike, said Mrs. Adams. The roofs and gutters leaked. The floors were spongy from the swampy wetness. The fireplace needed lighting to dry out the walls, but there was no firewood. The nearest water supply was almost five blocks away. It would be another thirty-three years before the house had running water and fifty-three years before a furnace was installed. There were no indoor bathrooms and no plumbing of any sort, nor would there be for seventy-eight years. The Adamses apparently shared the construction workers' outhouses. A telephone would go in before a bathroom. Baths were illegal from November to February in Philadelphia, where the Adamses had been living. In Boston, where they had lived earlier, baths were outlawed altogether, except on doctor's orders.

President Jefferson, who succeeded Adams, did not think much of the house either, perhaps because his design had been rejected. Jefferson said the place was "big enough for two emperors, one Pope and the Grand Lama." He did not reappoint Hoban, but named an English-born architect, Benjamin Henry Latrobe, to finish construction and to take charge of the Capitol Building job also. Latrobe had been in the United States only a few years but had designed some notable buildings in Philadelphia and Richmond. Latrobe offered his professional opinion of Hoban's house: "The north side is undistinguished, the south side is ill-proportioned, the ceiling has given way, and the smell from the open sewer is not a pleasant prologue to a visit to the President."

By the time of the War of 1812, Latrobe had finished twenty-three rooms. Two years later, on the evening of August 24, 1814, the British stormed into Washington and torched the mansion while President James Madison was away. By morning, only the walls were standing. The President's House was yet to have any symbolic meaning to America. The fire was minimized by the Washington *City Gazette:* "The destruction of the President's House cannot be said to be a great loss in one point of view, as we hope it will put an end to drawing rooms and levees; the resort of the idle, and the encouragers of spies and traitors."

Madison rehired Hoban to rebuild the house. The President lived nearby during the three-year reconstruction. Legend says that the name "White House" originated when workers painted the smoke-blackened walls white. Not so. The British order to burn the building had specifically referred to "the White House." Nobody knows when or how the name originated. White was traditional for houses of the style Hoban copied. Perhaps Washington himself named it after his wife's plantation, "White House," where he and Martha became engaged. Another possibility is that the mansion was painted white to set it apart from red brick houses in the Georgetown section of Washington. Whatever the origin, President Theodore Roosevelt made the name official in 1902.

Hoban died soon after completing the north and south porticoes. He was positive he had finished the White House. In a sense, he had. Despite changes by presidential families—adding rooms here, taking down an interior wall there—the outside of the White House proper remains almost exactly as Hoban built it. Inside, however, the mansion has undergone major and minor rebuildings and remodeling that reflect first-family tastes and the willingness of Congress to pay for them.

President James K. Polk added gas lights in 1848 to replace candles. President Franklin Pierce installed a hot-water system five years later. When Mrs. Mary Todd Lincoln overspent an appropriation for remodeling, President Lincoln said, "I'll pay for it out of my own pocket. It would stink in the nostrils of the American people to have it said that the President of the United States had approved a bill overruning an appropriation of $20,000 for flub-dubs for this damned old house, when the soldiers cannot have blankets." Congress nevertheless quietly paid the bill.

President Chester A. Arthur added an elevator in 1881. To raise money for new furnishings, he ordered twenty-four wagonloads of furniture and knickknacks from previous administrations to be hauled away and sold at auction. Jacqueline Kennedy reacquired many of them. Luckily, she said, President Arthur had not sold Lincoln's nine-foot-long solid rosewood bed. It was found in the White House basement; it was refurbished and returned to the second-floor Lincoln Room, one of the most famous in the White House. All White House discards now go to the Smithsonian Institution.

The White House was showing its age when President Ulysses S. Grant moved in. He called Army engineers to shore up sagging floors with timber supports. Rain and poor drainage had for years flooded the ground-floor kitchen. As the flooring decayed, new planking was nailed down on top of it. When the stink of rotten wood became overpowering, President Benjamin Harrison's wife ordered the entire floor replaced. Workers found a planking sandwich five layers thick and "enough cockroaches to populate the planet."

Since Lincoln's term, the White House had not been big enough to meet demands put on it as a presidential residence, for entertainment of dignitaries and as an executive office building. Mrs. Harrison suggested that a private residence be built nearby and the White House saved for ceremonial occasions. She had plans drawn for the addition of two enormous office wings which would have turned the White House into a U-shaped building. The public was appalled. It wanted no change in either the symbolic shape of the White House or its function as the official residence.

Mrs. Harrison's plan died in Congress, which did, however, vote money for White House "modernization, electrification and rat extermination." The White House was modernized and electrified, but rodents were still there as late as 1975, when a mouse was discovered near President Ford's office and another in the basement. Traps were baited with creamy peanut butter. A reporter asked the exterminator if the mice preferred creamy peanut butter to the crunchy variety. "Not that I know of," he said. "Creamy peanut butter is easier to apply, and the spoon is easier to clean."

President Theodore Roosevelt complained that the drafty White House was "a peril to health and even life itself." Floors had steadily sagged since Grant first noticed the problem thirty-three years earlier. Underpinnings were so wobbly that dishes rattled in State Dining Room cabinets when guests entered the room. There were mysterious creaking noises throughout the White House. Somebody said they were ghosts; and others passed them off as only mice. The White House also was a firetrap. Beams and studding were charred where electrical overloads had melted insulation.

Congress appropriated $500,000 for the second major rebuilding of the White House and construction of executive offices in the East and West wings. The entire eastern interior of the White House was torn out. Flooring was put in over new underpinnings reinforced with more than 170,000 bricks. Electrical and heating systems were replaced. The elevator was rebuilt with oak from trusswork taken from Boston's Old South Church, where raiders had gathered prior to the famous Tea Party.

Although contemporary accounts refer to the 1902 rebuilding as "The Restoration," architect Charles F. McKim was not overly proud of the job. President Roosevelt ordered the work done in less than five months. In the rush, wood chips and shavings were left in attics and became a fire hazard. Ceilings were slapdashed together with thousands of spikes driven into wet plaster. Floors quickly sagged again, and the ghostlike noises continued.

Soon the White House was ailing even worse than before. This time it was the rotten roof which needed immediate replacement, experts said, before it fell in on the President's head. President Coolidge disagreed. "I presume there are plenty of others who would be willing to take the risk of living under that roof." Three years into his administration, he changed his mind when he learned that a third floor could be added to provide more guest rooms, a solarium, and the sewing room that his wife wanted. Coolidge was only the first President to raise the roof of the White House.

On Christmas Eve, 1929, while President Herbert Hoover was dining, faulty wiring in the West Wing attic ignited the wood shavings. The blaze was fought by twenty-one fire companies. Hoover watched from the roof as firefighters dragged their hoses and ladders across the snow to combat the flames and prevent their invasion of the White House itself. Clearly, the White House needed overhauling, if not total rebuilding. But with World War II, the demand was for

Christmas Eve, 1929, fire in the White House was watched by President Hoover (roof at left). *The blaze was the worst in the White House since the British burned the building during the war of 1812.*

more office space. President Roosevelt added it, along with a bomb shelter whose exact location is still a secret.

On a summer night after the war, President Harry Truman stood on the lawn that sloped up toward the White House. Squinting toward the south portico, he calculated that the breeze coming in off the Potomac was being deflected upward by the slope and was hitting the White House at about the second-floor level. Truman decided he could enjoy the evening breeze if he built a second-floor balcony. Historians were appalled. So were architects, members of the Federal Commission on Fine Arts, Congressmen, and others who cried out against changing the outside of the White House. During the national fuss-and-feathers, Truman dipped into his discretionary fund and built the balcony anyway. The Treasury Department recalled all twenty-dollar bills and issued new ones showing the Truman balcony.

The White House was nearly 150 years old when President Truman moved in. The hodgepodge of changes and remodelings, often without regard to what the floors would support, had left the place in sorry condition. The White House had, moreover, seen hard use. Troops had occupied the East Room during the Civil War. President Lincoln's son had fired a toy cannon outside the Cabinet Room, and President James Garfield's son, Irving, had ridden his bicycle down the grand staircase. The nicks were still in the stone steps. President Theodore Roosevelt's son had scarred the wood floor in the East Room when he used it as a roller-skating rink until his mother caught him. Another son, Quentin, had taken his pony into the White House and up the elevator to cheer his brother Archie, who was in bed with the measles.

President Truman was puzzled by the strange nightly creakings, but not as alarmed by them as he was by the swaying chandelier in the Blue Room while he was receiving official visitors. Similar vibrations from above set the East Room ceiling and lamps to trembling. When the President played the piano, small piles of plaster dust settled on the floor of the room below. President Truman also discovered that his bathtub, directly over a reception room, was sinking into the flooring. He told newsmen he shocked Mrs. Truman by describing what would happen if he fell through the ceiling "wearing nothing but a bathtub while she was entertaining the Daughters of the American Revolution."

North-side view of the White House.

In January 1948 Truman asked architects to examine the mansion and suggest how it could be rebuilt from the ground up. A more drastic approach would be needed to save the White House. Hoban's sandstone walls were still good; the architects marveled at the masonry joints. Test borings showed that Hoban's foundations were set only five feet into clay. The only safe foundation lay twenty-five feet beneath the clay in an eighteen-foot-thick layer of gravel. The White House would have to be built *down* before it could be rebuilt *up.*

The heavy upper floors were, moreover, putting dangerous overloads on the ground floor, which, like a piece of Swiss cheese, was pocked with holes from electrical wiring, plumbing pipes, and heating conduits. Brickwork supporting the grand staircase was crumbling. The ceiling in the East Room was sagging six inches and could collapse at any time. Architects put stethoscopes to the walls and listened. Sure enough, the walls did creak—not from ghosts or mice, but from the weight of years of added plumbing, heating and other piping. Of grave concern was the Coolidge steel-and-tile roof. It was much too heavy to be safely supported by the decrepit building. The architects concluded that the White House was in serious danger of falling down. Editorial writers put it another way: The only thing that kept the White House standing was tradition.

Three solutions were proposed. Two would demolish the White House with a wrecker's ball and put up a new building. These were discarded in favor of the third idea, which was to rebuild, using Hoban's sandstone shell. In 1949 Congress appropriated $5,761,000 for the job. The Trumans moved into nearby Blair House, and work began December 7, 1949.

A team of 172 craftsmen was assembled. Inside and out, the mansion was webbed with scaffolding. Like a huge jigsaw puzzle, the White House was taken apart, piece by piece. Each was tagged as to location and sent to storage or to refurbishing studios. Some 95,000 bricks dating back to the Hoban era were shipped to Mount Vernon for restorational work on Washington's home.

Useless pieces were sent to nearby Fort Myer until somebody could figure out what to do with them. And then a most peculiar thing happened. The commanding officer of the fort began to receive letters from students and others requesting the junk as souvenirs. Congress quickly passed an act permitting the old pieces of the White House to be given away. For the cost of handling and shipping, thirteen kits were offered. They included a foot-long piece of lath for twenty-five cents, hand-forged spikes set in plastic, and a $100 build-your-own fireplace kit of White House bricks. More than 100,000 requests flooded Fort Myer. Only 30,000 could be filled.

As the White House was peeled away to its shell, char from the 1814 fire revealed structural dangers that were worse than suspected. Ripping away lath and plaster, workmen discovered gaps of from three to five inches between the inner and outer walls. Possibly alarmed at the prospect of public reaction over the White House being allowed to deteriorate to this extent, the government put a secret classification on photos of these conditions. The photos were not released until the fixup job was done.

With only Hoban's walls standing, the trickiest part of the rebuilding—the new foundation—began. A bulldozer scooped out ten thousand cubic yards of clay. The gaping hole under the White House would provide space to build two new basements for air condition-

South-side view of the White House showing the second-floor Truman Balcony.

ing, heating and other equipment, plus a utility area. With ironwork shoring up walls, pits four feet square were dug at intervals under Hoban's walls. The pits were sunk twenty-seven feet into the clay until they hit gravel. Concrete was poured into them. While it set, another series of pits was dug and poured. Eventually, 126 pits were cemented. The White House at last stood on a sturdy foundation.

Some 660 tons of steel beams and other structural members were jockeyed through Hoban's narrow doors and windows, raised, welded and riveted until they formed a skeleton which would independently support the new floors and walls. Heavy anchor bars joined the ironwork to the sandstone walls. Wood paneling was refinished to bring out its original luster. Interior decorators supervised details in every room. Only the Lincoln Room remained untouched.

Five automatic elevators were added, as was a fire-alarm system, conduits for future electrical and other utility additions, a central vacuum-cleaning system, running ice water and piped-in music for every room. Roosevelt's bomb shelter was refurbished with nine-foot-thick concrete walls, double steel doors, communications facilities, and a system for filtering out poison gas and radioactive dust. Finally, the roof was raised to permit the addition of fourteen guest rooms. The Trumans moved back in with assurances from architects that the White House would stand at least a century before another major reconstruction became necessary.

Today, the White House has about 235 furnished rooms, including about one hundred offices in the East and West wings, twenty-five bedrooms, three dining rooms, twenty baths, twenty-nine fireplaces, one hundred forty-seven windows, eight skylights, a bowling alley, a gymnasium, a library, a movie theater, a TV broadcasting room, a restaurant-sized kitchen, eight television antennae on the roof—one for each station in the Washington area—half a million feet of electrical wiring, more than 2,000 electrical outlets, 450 light fixtures, and a monthly electric bill in the thousands of dollars. The White House is surrounded by a seven-foot iron picket fence and thirteen gates. On the eighteen-acre grounds are a putting green, a tennis court, a helipad, fountains, flower gardens, shrubs, trees, a path for growing herbs for the President's chef, and an electronic squawker for scaring away birds.

To keep the White House operating requires a full-time staff of more than three hundred, including carpenters, painters, plumbers, thirty-four electricians, an upholsterer, a window washer, four housemen who wax and buff 600,000 square feet of wood floors, a corps of housekeepers who vacuum 15,000 square feet of carpeting and dust some of the world's most priceless antiques, and a battery of switchboard operators who answer the telephone when you dial 202-456-1414. Unless you have official business with somebody in the White House, do not call the number. The operators are too busy to handle unnecessary calls.

If you were able to buy the White House, it would cost more than $125 million, according to the Department of the Interior. To live in White House style, you would need an annual income of around $35 million. The annual cost of cutting the grass and keeping up the grounds comes to $200,000, half of what Hoban had estimated it would cost to build the place.

Future Presidents will continue to remodel and rebuild the White House as they try to make the house a home. One change will never be made. That is the prayer which President Franklin D. Roosevelt had carved on the State Dining Room mantel. It was written by President Adams the day after he moved in: "I pray Heaven to bestow the best of Blessings on this House and all that shall hereafter inhabit it. May none but honest and wise Men ever rule under this roof."

III

The Capitol Building

THE NATION'S CAPITOL BUILDING got into the shape it is in despite fallen arches, fires, explosions, a swaying dome, and a succession of temperamental builders who were sidewalk-superintended by Presidents and Congressmen looking over their shoulders and telling them how to do their job. Everybody seemed to feel his ideas were better than those of the amateur architect who designed the Capitol.

The building site, at that time the geographical center of Washington, was chosen by Pierre Charles L'Enfant, who laid out the city. The hill site had been a Powhatan Indian camp which L'Enfant described as "a pedestal waiting for a monument." In March 1792 Secretary of State Thomas Jefferson placed newspaper advertisements for contests to select the best designs for the Capitol and the White House. The Capitol was to contain fifteen rooms, including a Representatives' Hall holding three hundred and a smaller Senate room. The winner would get five hundred dollars or a gold medal. Judges were President George Washington, three District of Columbia commissioners, and Jefferson.

The contest drew only sixteen entries. Designs included a circus parade of men, animals, and eagles along the roof. One showed a dome topped with a huge rooster flapping his wings. The entry of Stephen Hallet, thirty-seven, a French-born architect, came close to winning. The judges asked him to try again. Three months after the contest ended, Dr. William Thornton, thirty-five, learned of it and got permission to submit a design. Thornton was a physician, but

The Capitol Building.

practicing medicine apparently was the least of his interests. Dr. Thornton's hobby was entering contests. He had won first prize in a design contest for the Philadelphia library. Horse racing was another interest. He parlayed his winnings into ownership of one of the fastest stables of thoroughbreds in the country.

Dr. Thornton's first design failed to win, but the judges were sufficiently impressed to ask him to try again. His second design was judged the winner, and he was awarded the five hundred dollars. Hoping to avoid offending Hallet, the judges awarded him an equal prize and hired him to evaluate Thornton's design and to prepare cost estimates. Thornton's drawing showed a building with two wings connected by a rotunda topped by a grapefruit-half-shaped dome. The north wing would house the Senate; the south, the Hall (now the House) of Representatives.

The professional architect Hallet took a look at the plans of the amateur architect Thornton and dismissed them as mere "exhibi-

East Front of the Capitol of the United States as originally designed by William Thornton — and adopted by General Washington, President of the United States.

Dr. William Thornton, an amateur architect, drew this design for the Capitol. President Washington was impressed, and Thornton's design won first prize in the national competition.

tions." Hallet said the building was impractical, would take too long to build and be too costly. Hallet and Thornton set to feuding, and President Washington appointed a commission to resolve the matter. Three of the members were contest losers, including Hallet. The others were Thornton and architect James Hoban, who had won the prize for designing the White House. Now there were three and sometimes four critics picking Thornton's design to pieces. The ever-persistent Hallet meanwhile drew more designs in hopes of knocking out Thornton's, but none caught the fancy of Washington or Jefferson.

A key point of disagreement was Thornton's rotunda. Hallet wanted a square court rather than a round one. President Washington at last told Hallet to get on with the job of building the Capitol; the rotunda issue could be settled later. Construction began, and Congress set a completion date of 1800, when the capital would be moved from Philadelphia. In a Masonic ceremony, on September 18, 1793, the cornerstone was laid by President Washington, who wore a Masonic apron said to have been embroidered by the wife of General Marquis de Lafayette, the French general who joined Washington's army and fought for America during the Revolution.

Ignoring the President's order to postpone the rotunda, Hallet laid foundations for a square court. How he got as far with them as he did without Thornton's apparent knowledge is a mystery. When Washington showed up at the site, as he frequently did to offer suggestions, he discovered the court. The President was furious. District commissioners reprimanded Hallet, who quit. They refused his resignation; then, determined to have the final say, they fired him. Hallet walked off the job and took the building plans with him. The commissioners sued for the return of the plans. Thornton, meanwhile, yanked out the square foundations.

Construction had not progressed beyond the Senate wing foundations when George Hadfield, thirty-one, an English-born architect, was put in charge. Hopes that fresh leadership would speed the job were dashed when Hadfield renewed the attacks on Thornton's design. Washington and Jefferson disagreed with him. It was Hadfield's turn to quit; he reconsidered, however, and withdrew his resignation, but he continued to snipe as construction poked along for three years. Costs were higher than expected, just as Hallet had predicted. Building funds were running low, and Congress voted to borrow up to $300,000.

George Blagden, superintendent of stonework and quarrying, could find few skilled stonemasons and bricklayers. Slave labor was leased from nearby plantations. Bonus pay lured artisans from Philadelphia, Baltimore, Richmond, and New England who found the building site was hot and humid in summer and rainy and snowy in winter. Sandstone for facing the interior brick walls was barged via the Potomac River from Virginia's Aquia quarries, which were supplying the White House job. Kilns and mortar puddles pocked Capitol Hill. Trees were felled in nearby forests and dressed into lumber.

By the spring of 1798 the exterior walls of the 126-by-120-foot boxy wing were nine feet shy of their planned 41-foot height. Interior brick walls had been completed, the roof was framed, and wooden shingles were being prepared. Hadfield decided to add an attic. He was overruled, and he quit again. He reconsidered, but by this time the commissioners had had enough: they fired him. Hoban was made building superintendent of both the Capitol and the White House. Hoban and Thornton worked well together, but so much time had been lost that only the Senate wing was done by November 17, 1800, when the government moved to Washington.

Into that north wing crowded 32 Senators and 106 Representatives. To ease crowding, a temporary one-story building was put up on the site of the south wing. The brick building was connected to the senatorial wing by a covered passageway. Representatives moved into it in the winter of 1801, but in the heat of the following summer the sweltering Congressmen named it "the Oven." While they baked in the Oven and fretted over the snail's-pace progress on their wing, Jefferson, now President, appointed Benjamin Latrobe, thirty-nine, to take charge of Capitol construction.

Jefferson, himself an architect, was an admirer of Latrobe, whose talents seemed boundless. He had designed schools, churches, Virginia's state capitol, banks, Philadelphia's first water system, and a Richmond prison featuring a new concept of solitary confinement. Most of all, Latrobe liked to build canals. To Latrobe, building the Capitol was just another job. He hired architect John Lenthal, gave him almost total responsibility for day-to-day decisions, and left Washington to build the Chesapeake and Delaware Canal.

Before he left, Latrobe said Thornton's design was an abomination, and he gave Jefferson his ideas for improving it. Change the design of the Hall of Representatives, said Latrobe; make it circular. Raise the floor of the Senate to make room for the Supreme Court. Make the Capitol face east instead of west, as Thornton had laid it out. Exactly why he thought the direction should be changed is not clear, but he convinced Jefferson, and the changes were ordered. Dr. Thornton had more than met his match in Latrobe. Fighting a losing battle to keep his design intact, Thornton was put in charge of the Patent Office by Jefferson. That job, the President believed, would keep him away from the Capitol construction site.

By the summer of 1804 the south wing exterior was done to the height of the main floor. The Representatives moved back into the senatorial wing and were constantly bothered by construction noises, including those of the demolition of the Oven. Building progress continued to lag, and long-smoldering discontent with Latrobe's absences erupted in Congress.

Latrobe could not be bothered to leave the canal to answer critics, but he did fire back a letter. He said that the slow progress was not his fault, but rather that of nit-picking Congressmen. He lectured them on the headaches of building supplies and labor. The heavy de-

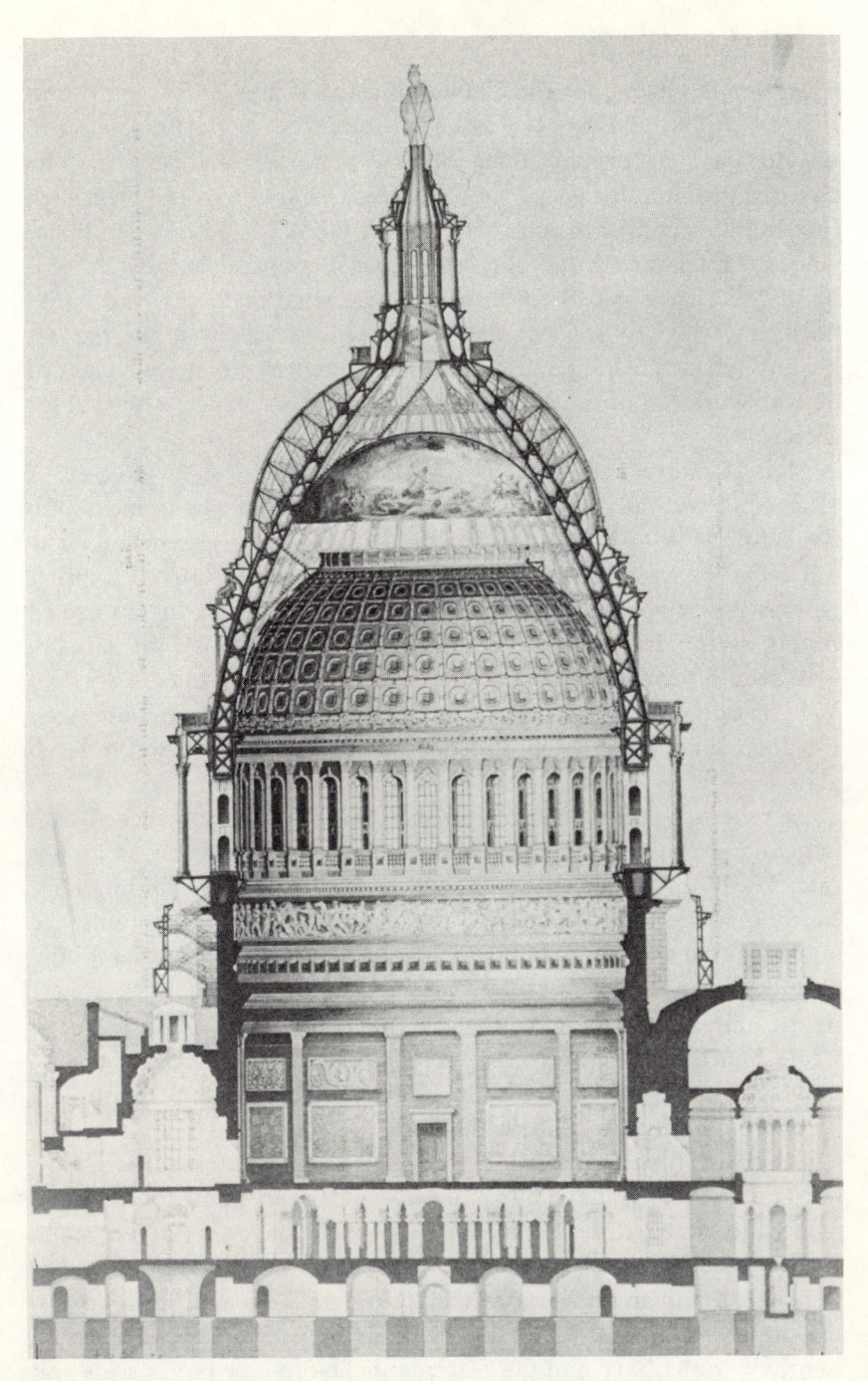

Architectural design of the ironwork that forms the upper dome of the Capitol.

mand for sandstone for the Capitol and the White House was draining the Aquia quarries. It was becoming increasingly time-consuming to find larger and finer blocks. Congressional funding, he charged, was too little, too slow, and came too late in the year, considering that he had to contract for slave labor by January 1. "Those who are afterward hired are few, expensive and generally inferior hands." Latrobe said the fishing season started in March and lasted until mid-May. As soon as the fishing season was over, the harvest began. Between fishing and harvesting, there was not much chance of getting work out of the paid laborers, and the slaves were needed for the crops.

Many Congressmen were not satisfied with Latrobe's excuses. A House bill was introduced to abandon the Capitol and to move into the White House. The President could rent a house somewhere. The bill failed to pass. President Jefferson, meanwhile, stirred another tempest by suggesting that Latrobe change his design for a paneled ceiling in the House chamber. Jefferson said that a hundred panes of glass would provide better lighting. Latrobe refused; the glass would leak, he said, and the skylight would cast a crazy quilt of shadows on the floor. Jefferson insisted. Latrobe was stubborn. Jefferson ordered glass.

Latrobe told Lenthal to ignore the President and to proceed with paneling. Jefferson's reaction when he saw the paneling was no less than Washington's when he learned of Hallet's square foundations. Latrobe was by now back on the canal, so Lenthal became the scapegoat. In a scathing letter to Lenthal, the President ordered him to pull as many workers as were required off whatever jobs they were doing and immediately to replace the panels with glass. Latrobe wrote Lenthal: "You and I are both blockheads. Presidents are the only architects. Therefore, let us fall down and worship them. God bless thee. Be moderate with the lime."

Other problems arose after the Hall of Representatives was finished in 1807. To Latrobe's embarrassment and Thornton's amusement, the changed design made for poor acoustics in the chamber. Nothing solved the problem. Elsewhere, masonry arches were weakening and in some cases collapsing under loads. Latrobe dismissed the problem. "I'm sorry the arches have fallen," he told Lenthal, "but I have had these accidents before on a larger scale and must therefore grin and bear it."

Stone and other building materials clutter the grounds around the Capitol as construction proceeds.

When still another and larger arch cracked, Latrobe wrote that he was "horror-struck," but not sufficiently so to come to Washington to find a solution. Less than eight weeks later, arches collapsed under the Senate floor, and Lenthal was killed by falling masonry. Latrobe investigated and said the cause was due to Congress-imposed haste and economies in construction. Henceforth, said Latrobe, he would build at a pace and quality that his expertise decided. Congress seemed to agree with him.

At the outbreak of the War of 1812, the Capitol was U-shaped. Domes and cupolas capped the north and south wings, which were connected by a columned passageway. On August 24, 1814, British troops burned the Capitol and the White House. Congress debated whether to move the capital from Washington, but decided to stay.

While rebuilding, Latrobe designed a new semicircular Hall of Representatives, which he was confident would solve the acoustic problems of the old. Progress was severely hampered by the sandstone shortage, and Congress continued to fume over Latrobe's frequent absences. Late in 1817, Latrobe quit during another dispute and was replaced by architect Charles Bulfinch, fifty-five, of Boston, a friend of President James Monroe.

Bulfinch saw little need to improve on Latrobe's design for the central rotunda area. He prepared several alternative sketches for the dome and submitted them to President Monroe and his Cabinet. Bulfinch purposely drew one of them for a 145-foot-high dome. He considered this design absurd, but submitted it for comparison purposes with the dome he favored. Bulfinch was flabbergasted when his worst design was picked over the others. Try as he would, he could not persuade the President to choose the smaller dome.

During construction of the rotunda under the projected dome, a basement crypt was built to hold the body of President Washington. Although he was buried at Mount Vernon, his widow, Martha, had given permission to move the body to the Capitol. The rotunda floor was built with a circular opening so that visitors could look down into the crypt. But Martha Washington had died, and relatives refused to remove the President's body from beside his wife's. The opening was sealed, but the crypt remains.

The $687,000 reconstruction job proceeded as fast as appropriations and building materials permitted. The only somber note was a cave-in which killed Blagden, who had supervised Capitol stonework for nearly a quarter century. With the wooden dome covered by copper sheathing and both wings virtually complete, Congress moved back fifteen years after the 1814 burning.

Representatives discovered that not only was the sound problem as bad as before, but the Hall had become an acoustical freak. It is said that John Quincy Adams first discovered the peculiarity when he became a Representative after serving as President. From his seat he could hear political opponents whispering, even though they were fifty feet from him. Present-day visitors to the Hall, now National Statuary Hall, can themselves hear people whispering on the other side of the room.

Congress had no control over the rotunda's use in the 1850s. It became a flea market where hucksters hawked "stoves, stew pans, pianos, mouse traps, and watch ribbons, while an impresario set up a 'Panorama of Paris, Admission 50 cents.'" On January 30, 1835, President Andrew ("Old Hickory") Jackson was leaving the crowded rotunda when a madman fired a pistol at him. The shot misfired. The President attacked the assailant with his cane, and the gunman pulled another pistol from his cloak. It too misfired, and a Navy lieutenant decked him. This was the first assassination attempt against a U.S. President.

By 1850, the Capitol was too small to meet the needs of 62 Senators and 232 Representatives. The proposal to build extensions on the north and south wings was led by a Mississippi Senator named Jefferson Davis, who was to become President of the Southern Confederacy during the Civil War. More than at any time in the past, Congressmen interested themselves in construction details and decided that more durable marble would be preferable to soft sandstone. Marble was chosen from Lee, Massachusetts, quarries. Dolomite, another form of marble, came from Conoly's Quarry near Baltimore.

Construction under Thomas U. Walter, forty-six, a master bricklayer, draftsman, and self-taught architect, was delayed by a fire that destroyed nearly half the Library of Congress, which was housed in the Capitol at that time. When Davis became War Secretary in 1853, he took overall supervision of construction and appointed Army Captain of Engineers Montgomery C. Meigs to work with Walter. The House occupied its present hall in 1857, and the Senate moved into its room two years later. The Supreme Court took over the old Senate room. In 1897 the Library of Congress occupied its own building, and in 1935 the Supreme Court moved to its present location near the Capitol.

Thanks to Walter's fireproofing, the Capitol suffered only minor damage from two gas explosions and fires. But that was before 5:13 P.M., Sunday, November 6, 1898. Only a few guards were in the building when illuminating gas leaking from a four-inch main in the old Senate basement exploded and touched off a fire. The blast demolished the Supreme Court room and library, blew out doors and windows, dropped arches, collapsed thick marble floors, and bulged a wall. Damage was more than $250,000. In time for the American

Bicentennial celebration in 1976, the old Supreme Court was restored to its appearance before the Civil War. Workers stripped away more than a quarter inch of paint from the sandstone walls and refinished them in the original honey color.

Before the Capitol extensions were completed, it was realized that they would dwarf the Bulfinch rotunda. Therefore, Congress decided to demolish the rotunda and build the taller one we know today. With Latrobe's sandstone walls as a base, Walter designed a drum-shaped masonry-and-cast-iron structure encircled by marble columns. On top of this open drum would fit a twin-shelled dome of iron, painted white to harmonize with the rest of the building. Capping the dome would be a fifty-foot-tall circular lantern, also surrounded by columns. The lantern would be crowned by a statue.

Because most of the statues in the Capitol had been done by Italians, it was decided that an American should get the commission. Thomas Crawford, a New Yorker living in Rome, was selected. Crawford had served his apprenticeship as a tombstone cutter and had done figures of Jefferson and Patrick Henry. Crawford's 19½-foot statue of a woman stood on a ball supported by a pedestal. He intended her to wear a liberty cap modeled after those of emancipated slaves in ancient Rome. Amid the growing debate between North and South over slavery, Davis ordered Crawford to make another cap. That the sculptor substituted an eagle's head with long feathers accounts for the popular idea that the statue is of Pocahontas, daughter of Powhatan, head of the Algonquin tribes.

Crawford's Statue of Freedom was shipped to the United States in five plaster molds. On reaching Washington, the sections were hauled to Clark Mills's foundry in Bladensburg, Maryland, where there was a master craftsman who could make bronze castings from plaster. It is believed that his name was Philip Reed, an emancipated slave. The finished statue weighed seven and a half tons and was taken to the Capitol and displayed while the dome was being built.

Preparatory to building the dome, Captain Meigs put up a scaffolding tower with a derrick on top. The rig was placed in the center of the rotunda floor. Power was supplied by steam-driven engines which also operated another derrick on the roof of the old Senate wing. The derricks lifted the long twenty-three-ton marble columns and ironwork into place.

Stonemasons working in tents in front of the Capitol hollowed out

Capitol construction was stopped before the Civil War, but President Lincoln ordered the work resumed. "If people see the Capitol going on, it will be a sign to them that we intend the Union shall go on," he said.

the columns which, in addition to forming the peristyle around the drum, would serve as chimneys for Capitol fireplaces. Embedded in the drum's top rim were two-and-a-half-ton iron brackets. Riveted to them were the thirty-six iron ribs forming the dome's skeleton. To the ribs were riveted hundreds of iron panels. Intricate trusswork connected the inner and outer domes. More than ten thousand pieces of iron fittings were drawn to precise specifications and made in James Bogardus's mill in New York City.

Construction stopped before the Civil War started, but President Abraham Lincoln ordered work resumed. "If people see the Capitol going on, it will be a sign to them that we intend the Union shall go on," Lincoln said. Except for wartime delays in material, progress was good. Early in the war, the Capitol was turned into a barracks for three thousand Union soldiers. A military bakery was built in the basement, with flour being stored in Washington's crypt. The Capitol was later turned into a military hospital with fifteen hundred beds.

On Wednesday, December 2, 1863, the dome was ready to receive the Statue of Freedom. During a celebration attended by Lincoln, the derrick raised Freedom's head up through the eye of the dome. In twenty minutes, workers bolted it in place as American flags were unfurled and cannon on Capitol Hill boomed one shot for each state above and below the Mason-Dixon Line. Artillery at a dozen Union fortifications surrounding Washington thundered thirty-five-gun answers.

When the dome was completed in 1865, the year the Civil War ended, Constantino Brumidi, a naturalized citizen who had fled political persecution in Italy, began his famous rotunda fresco, *Apotheosis* (Glorification) *of George Washington.* Brumidi, who had restored Vatican art, did much of his work in the eye of the dome while lying on his back on scaffolding 180 feet above the rotunda floor. To the copper surface of the underdome he applied pigments to freshly troweled mortar. Chemical changes as the mortar set enhanced the coloring. The fresco covers 4,664 square feet and includes Washington flanked by goddesses of liberty and victory and thirteen maidens representing the original states. Brumidi often is called the American Michelangelo.

Brumidi then began a three-hundred-foot-long frieze high up around the rotunda cornice. On a day when nobody else was in the rotunda, he was working on his seventh panel, *Penn's Treaty with the Indians,* when his chair slipped. The seventy-four-year-old artist would have plunged to his death on the floor below had he not caught hold of a scaffolding rung. Brumidi dangled helplessly for fifteen minutes until his screams were heard by a watchman who pulled him to safety. But the emotional shock brought on an asthma attack, and Brumidi died. The remaining panels were finished by others.

Except for restorations and renovations, the Capitol remained substantially unchanged until 1959, when Congress decided to extend the east front of the building to add more than fifty offices, with House and Senate dining rooms. As it stands today, the Capitol is 751 feet long, 350 feet wide, and rises 287 feet, five and a half inches

Bronze "Statue of Freedom" atop the Capitol is believed to have been cast by an emancipated slave. Eagle's head and long feathers have led to the popular but false notion that the statue is of Pocahontas, daughter of the Powhatan Indian chief.

from the base of the east front to the top of the Statue of Freedom's helmet. The Capitol contains about 540 rooms covering sixteen and a half acres of floor space.

The dome weighs nearly nine million pounds and cost more than $1 million to build. It sways as much as four inches as it moves clockwise with the sun. At sunrise, the dome swings south. During the day it moves southwest, then west as the sun sets. The dome returns to its original position at nightfall. The lantern in the dome is traditionally lit when either house of Congress is in night session. In 1960 workmen inspecting the Statue of Freedom discovered a nest of bees in her feathered bonnet.

In 1965 more than twenty-one major and a thousand minor cracks were discovered in the sandstone face of the west wall of the old Capitol wings. Experts warned that a mild sonic boom could cause the wall to come crashing down. Architect J. George Stewart proposed to extend the back of the building up to eighty-eight feet, thus correcting the problem and adding more than a hundred offices. But, as has happened throughout the life of the Capitol, critics and supporters mounted attacks and counterattacks. The back of the Capitol still stands, cracked and bulging more than four inches. House and Senate committees continue to argue whether to repair or to extend the wall. That debate would have given Doctor Thornton great satisfaction.

IV

Washington National Monument

IT IS HARD TO BELIEVE that the majestically simple Washington National Monument could have taken a century to build, a period spanning the terms of twenty-one United States Presidents.

Most monuments honor somebody who is dead. George Washington, Commander-in-Chief of the American Revolutionary War army, was alive and had yet to be elected President when the Continental Congress proposed the idea of erecting a monument in his honor. Meeting August 7, 1783, in the capital at Trenton, New Jersey, the Congressmen voted to build a bronze statue to be placed in the permanent nation's capital whenever it was built.

The concept for the statue was not at all how we picture Washington today. He was to be wearing a dress, similar to those of ancient Greeks, while sitting on a horse. He would be holding a truncheon something like a policeman's billy. Crowning his head was to be a laurel wreath. Artistic license being what it was in those days, Washington did not object.

When the Congressmen picked the townsite, they chose architect Pierre Charles L'Enfant to lay it out. He planned the monument for a marshy patch of ground south of the White House. Washington, now President, objected to building the statue with public funds, which were already low. The plan was dropped.

Nine days after Washington's death in 1799, Representative (later Chief Justice of the United States) John Marshall revived the idea. Congress voted to build a mausoleum of American granite and marble. It was to be pyramid-shaped and stand a hundred feet square at the base. Washington's body was in a marble vault at the Mount Vernon, Virginia, family estate. His widow, Martha, reluctantly agreed, "at a sacrifice of individual feeling . . . to a sense of public duty," to remove the body to the capital. However, a bill to fund the mausoleum failed in the Senate.

Washington was eleven years in the memory of Congressmen when the monument question came up again. Attitudes had changed: now the monument was opposed. If you were of Washington's political persuasions, you wanted the monument. If not, it was more fitting, said Representative Erastus Root of New York, that "Washington's name live in history [rather] than in marble." Said George Cary of Georgia, "We need no monuments [to Washington]. . . . He has a monument in the heart of every American."

While Congress twiddled for six more years, Virginia lawmakers proposed to build a tomb for Washington in Richmond. To head off the possibility of our first President being memorialized in any place but Washington, Congress debated the mausoleum idea again and ordered one to be built in the Capitol Building. The spot chosen was below the dome and rotunda and under the floor of the crypt. Here Washington would be entombed. Or so Congress thought.

They had not bargained on two things. First, Martha Washington was now dead for fourteen years and in the vault beside her husband. Moreover, relatives recalled Washington's will, which instructed that he be buried at Mount Vernon. Congress nevertheless asked John Augustine Washington, Washington's grandnephew and the owner of Mount Vernon, to permit removal of both bodies to the Capitol. The grandnephew refused, and the monument idea faltered.

In 1832 Senator Henry Clay of Kentucky brought up the monument question again. By now, a 150-foot circular column monument to Washington had been standing in Baltimore for three years, a fact which embarrassed some Congressmen. Designed by a young architect, Robert Mills, the monument rested on a squarish base. A statue of Washington stood at the top of the column. Why put up a second monument? a number of Congressmen asked. Senator Clay's eloquence prevailed. A group of prominent Washingtonians decided to get on with the job. Meeting in the City Hall on September 26, 1833, they formed the Washington National Monument Society. Chief Justice Marshall was elected president and George Watterson,

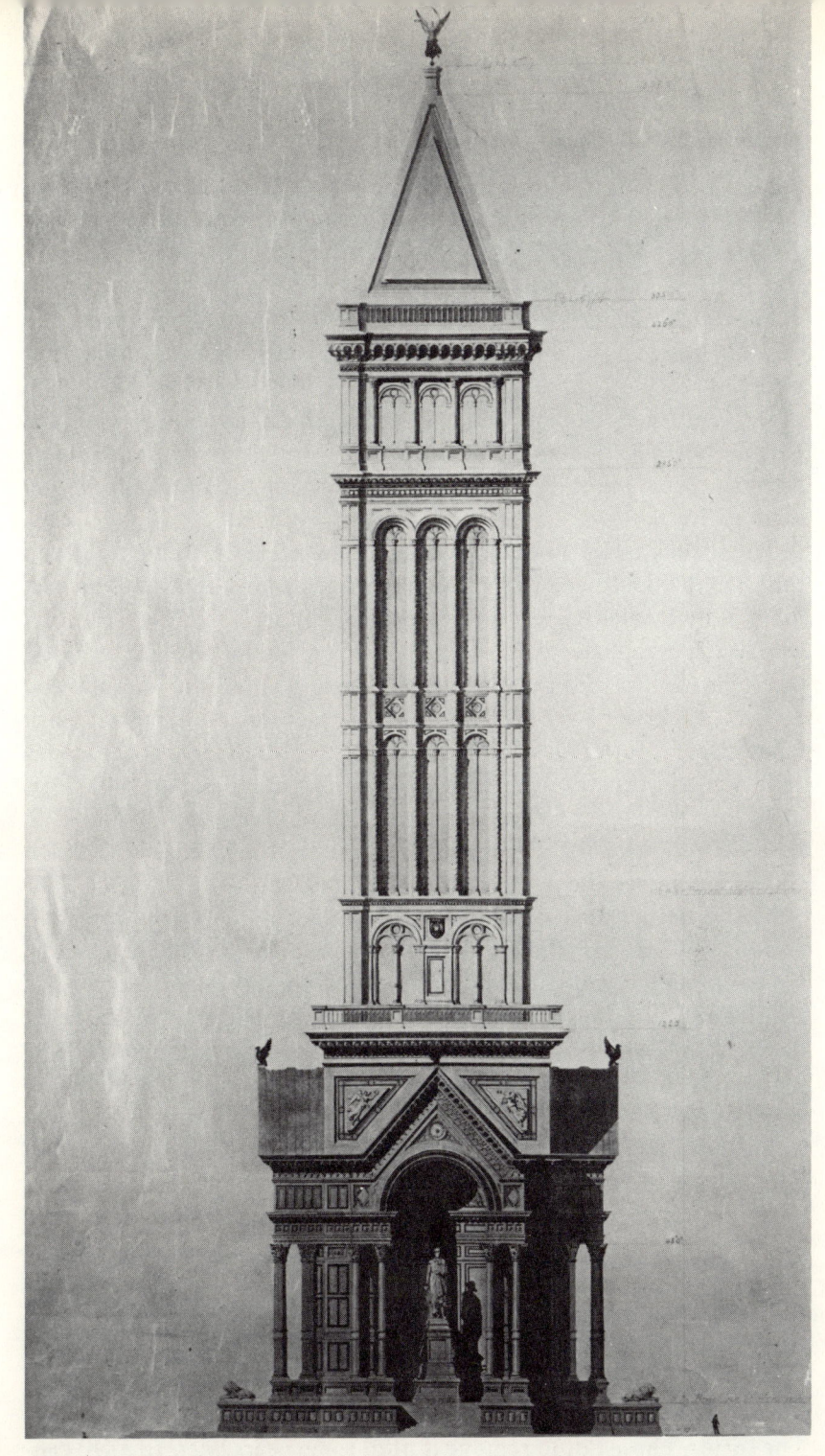

Designer M. P. Hapgood's "cathedral" plan for the Washington National Monument.

librarian of Congress, was named secretary. The society decided to build a monument through public subscriptions, none exceeding one dollar a year. The organization thought the monument should represent a gift from the American people.

Funds were collected through agents who were paid ten cents commission, which was later raised to fifteen cents for each dollar collected. Contributions ranged from a high of $6,391.19 in Ohio, where sheriffs collected, to a low of $31.95 by politically appointed agents in Vermont. Collections were hindered by criticism of some society members who were accused of being more interested in promoting their political views than in building a monument.

The society advertised for architectural sketches in 1836, by which time $28,000 had been raised. Many designs were submitted, including one by Daniel Ramee that resembled France's Arch of Triumph, which was completed that year. The society finally selected a design by Robert Mills, who that same year was appointed the nation's first Federal Architect by President Andrew Jackson. Mills, a native of Charleston, South Carolina, had served as a draftsman for Thomas Jefferson and became known for his work on other capital buildings, including the Patent Office, the Treasury Building, and the old U.S. Post Office. Mills also designed the Bunker Hill Monument, which closely resembles the Washington Monument.

Mills's design was a blend of Greek, Babylonian and Egyptian architecture. He saw the monument as a national pantheon, an enormous circular, temple-like building. Around the outer ring of the pantheon would be statues of signers of the Declaration of Independence and Revolutionary War heroes, including Washington. Mills planned a tomb at the base of the monument should it ever be decided to move Washington's body. Thirty stone columns, twelve feet in diameter and thirty feet tall, would support the pantheon's roof. Perched on the roof over the main entrance would be a statue of Washington wearing a toga and driving a horse-drawn chariot. Rising from the center of the pantheon was to be an obelisk, a four-sided pillar that tapered gradually until it formed a pyramid at the top. Mills planned a vertical railway to carry visitors to an observatory within the pyramid.

With the public better visualizing what was planned, fund-raising surged, but was hampered by the dollar-a-year donation restriction. The society chose not to remove it until some years later. In 1840 census takers were given the added duty of soliciting money. Later, U.S. deputy marshals made solicitations. Donors were given two sizes of souvenir lithographs and portraits of Washington. The census takers pocketed twenty cents commission for each dollar collected.

By 1848 some $87,000 had been accumulated. The following year, nearly half a century after Washington's death, Congress granted a site. The thirty-seven-acre area was the same one shown in L'Enfant's plan for the statue. Soil tests, however, showed the location to be too marshy, so a knoll one hundred yards east of the original site was chosen. This site was ideal, as it afforded an excellent view of the capital. Building stone and sand could easily be brought by barge or by the Baltimore and Susquehanna Railroad from nearby quarries. The finely grained white marble would come from Thomas Symington's quarry near Baltimore, eleven miles northeast. Symington donated the 24,500-pound block of marble for the cornerstone, and the railroads hauled it free to Washington.

Sunday, July 4, 1848, the day selected for laying the cornerstone, dawned sunny. A light early-morning rain had "laid the dust and infused a delicious freshness in the air," as one historian later put it. Railroads and stagecoach lines into the city reduced their rates for the occasion. A crowd of between fifteen thousand and twenty thousand gathered near the site and along the parade route from the Capitol Building. Many purchased reserved seats in awning-covered bleachers put up around a temporary arch that stood over the site. The arch was draped in red, white, and blue bunting. Tethered to its top and glowering out on the crowd was a huge American eagle which was said to be forty years old.

President James K. Polk led the parade to the site. His carriage was followed by those of his Cabinet, Congressmen, and marching groups that included the Marlborough Cavalry, the Eagle Artillerists of Baltimore, the Washington Light Infantry, the Marine Corps Band, and seven volunteer fire companies. The horse-drawn steam pumpers and hose carts were resplendent with flowers, flags and bunting. The firefighters wore their companies' distinctive dress uniforms, ranging from red jackets to white pantaloons. Various Indian organizations, fraternal societies, and antialcohol temperance groups brought up the rear. Among honored guests were Dolley Madison, widow of President James Madison; Alexander Hamilton's widow; and Martha Washington's grandson, George Washington Parke

Robert Mills's original design of the Washington National Monument would have stood 600 feet high.

Custis. Barely noticed was a little-known Congressman, Abraham Lincoln.

The main speech was given by Robert C. Winthrop, Speaker of the House of Representatives, who was the society's third choice. Their first pick was former President John Quincy Adams, who turned them down because of ill health. Next they tried Daniel Webster, but he pleaded "pressure of business and shortness of time to prepare a speech."

The cornerstone-laying ceremony followed Speaker Winthrop's two-hour oration. In a zinc case were placed numerous mementoes, including copies of the Declaration of Independence and the Constitution, a portrait of Washington, all national coins of the time, an American flag, newspapers from cities in fourteen states, including the Worcester (Massachusetts) *Palladium,* the Williamsport (Pennsylvania) *Lycoming Gazette,* and the Fincastle (Virginia) *Valley Whig.* Other memorabilia were *Maury's Wind and Current Charts of the North Atlantic, Appleton's Railroad and Steamboat Companion,* the bylaws of Powhatan Tribe Number One, and a copy of the constitution of the first organized temperance society in America.

The cornerstone was laid by Grand Master Benjamin B. French of the Grand Lodge of Free and Accepted Masons, Washington. French wore the Masonic apron and sash that had belonged to President Washington. He used the same Mason's hammer Washington had used in laying the Capitol Building cornerstone on September 18, 1783. After applying the Masonic square, level and plumb to the northeast corner, French pronounced the cornerstone sound. He next poured a vial of corn while invoking "the blessing of plenty upon the nation"; a vial of wine, symbolizing the "joy ever to be found in our broad land"; and a vial of oil, "the healing oil of consolation." Although the cornerstone was a milestone in the progress of the monument, nobody has since been able to single out this stone from the other blocks of weathered marble. Its exact location is a mystery.

Construction began with the appointment of Superintendent David Hepburn, who hired a small work force to lay a 6,400-square-foot foundation for the obelisk. The pantheon itself would have to await more money. Blocks of blue gneiss rock weighing up to eight tons each, brought in from Potomac Valley quarries, were cemented into a flat-topped pyramid. The foundation was eighty feet square and extended seven feet eight inches below ground, and fifteen feet eight inches above.

The cornerstone ceremony focused new attention on the project. "Give-a-Penny" appeals went out to the nation's three million schoolchildren. But donations totaled only $230,000, far short of the $1,250,000 Mills had estimated would be required. In lieu of money, Alabama offered a decorative stone. The idea struck the fancy of the society, which invited other states to appropriately inscribe and contribute a "block of marble or other durable stone, a product of its soil." The size was to approximate that of the monument's slabs, four feet long, two feet high, and from twelve to to eighteen inches thick. The invitation was later extended to foreign governments, a gesture which nearly doomed the monument.

One of the foreign stones contributed was a gift from Pope Pius IX. The stone came from Rome's Temple of Concord. The gift infuriated the American Party, a political organization popularly called the "Know-Nothings." The group was somewhat secretive, and its leaders, when asked questions about their hostility to foreign-born Americans and to Catholics, said that they "knew nothing." The Pope's stone, vowed the Know-Nothings, would never become part of the Washington Monument.

Early in the morning of Monday, March 6, 1854, the night watchman at the monument was approached by four to ten men. He later told police they surrounded his hut and piled stones against the door. The intruders took the Pope's stone, put it in a handcart, and vanished. The watchman was unable to explain why he did not drive off the intruders with his shotgun, or why he waited at least two hours to fire the gun to sound an alarm. The society fired him. A one-hundred-dollar reward was posted for the return of the stone and information leading to the arrest of the thieves. The stone was never recovered, and no arrests were made. It was probably dumped into the nearby Potomac River.

The incident disgusted many Americans. Contributions fell off sharply. The society appealed to Congress, which voted to appropriate $200,000 on Washington's Birthday, 1855. On the evening before the appropriation, a group of more than 750 Know-Nothings, many of whom had infiltrated the society, called a meeting. They voted in seventeen of their own officers. The next morning they announced they were "in possession of" the Washington Monument. The outraged House of Representatives immediately acted to halt the appropriation. It would be twenty-one more years before Congress would again vote funds for the Washington Monument. Two weeks after the Know-Nothings' coup, another blow fell when architect Robert Mills died in his Capitol Hill home.

The Know-Nothings fumbled along with construction but laid only thirteen courses—twenty-six feet—of marble, although the stone had been declared unsuitable. Their fund-raising was similarly inept: during the next ten months they collected only $51.66. Two years later the Know-Nothing movement collapsed. Its leaders returned possession of the monument to the society together with a treasury of only $285.09. To prevent repetition of the debacle, Congress in 1859 incorporated the society. National fund-raising began afresh. Post office collection points were set up, and solicitations were made at election polls when Abraham Lincoln was being voted into his first term as President. Overall results were disappointing. With the imminent War Between the States, Washington was no longer first in the hearts of his countrymen. In 1861 only $88.52 was raised throughout the nation, including fifteen cents in Mississippi and forty-eight cents in Washington's native Virginia.

At the start of the Civil War, the monument stood at about 176 feet. It looked like a hollow, oversized chimney and remained that way during the war. Monument grounds became grazing fields for beef cattle, which were slaughtered there to provide meat for Union troops. The grounds also were used for exercises by the Union Army.

Fifteen years later the society began anew, only to meet strong opposition to the idea of finishing the monument. The nation's esthetic tastes had changed. To many Congressmen, the Mills design was a horror. There was speculation that the monument's foundations were crumbling with age. The society nevertheless proceeded on the Fourth of July with a national appeal for funds. "The appeal for a Fourth of July contribution . . . will not amount to much," predicted the New York *Tribune*. "Public judgment on that abortion has been made up. The country has failed in many ways to honor the memory of its first President, but the neglect to finish this monument is not to be reckoned among them. A wretched design, a wretched location, and an insecure foundation match well with its empty treasury. If the public will let the big furnace chimney on the Potomac Flats alone, and give its energies instead to cleaning out morally and

Oxen hauled marble slabs to the construction site of the Washington National Monument in this drawing from a periodical, Gleason's Pictorial, *January 7, 1854.*

physically the city likewise named after the Father of this Country, it will better honor his memory."

But the United States was in the midst of its Centennial celebration, and the mood of the nation was for resumption of construction. Congress appropriated $200,000, and the society intensified fundraising efforts. Completion was targeted for five years later, on the 1871 centennial of General Charles Cornwallis's surrender to George Washington at Yorktown and the end of the War of Independence. The target would be missed by four years.

President Ulysses S. Grant personally picked Lieutenant Colonel Thomas Lincoln Casey to finish the monument. Colonel Casey, a huge hulk of a man with salt-and-pepper hair and a walrus mustache, quickly found his task complicated by problems on every side. Years of neglect had made the site a blight of dilapidated shanties. Rains turned the grounds into a muddy quagmire. Thieves had stolen some of the marble. The outside scaffolding needed replacement, and the rope used to haul supplies up the inside of the shaft to the 176-foot level had been pulled down.

Colonel Casey solved the rope problem by tying several hundred feet of threadlike wire to a pigeon's leg. The pigeon was turned loose inside the shaft, and a shotgun was fired. The frightened pigeon flew up and out of the top. The bird was then shotgunned out of the sky and the wire recovered. Workmen tied twine of increasing thickness to the wire. Pulling them through the opening at the top of the monument, they finally were able to haul out a heavy lifting rope.

Test borings confirmed that the foundation was unsafe to support the monument's weight. The Corps of Engineers enlarged the area to two and a half times the original size. They dug $13\frac{1}{2}$ feet deeper until the foundation was only two feet above the high-tide level of the Potomac. The new $126\frac{1}{2}$-foot-square foundation extended 36 feet 10 inches into the ground and rested on a two-foot-thick bed of fine sand, clay, and gravel. The underpinning of the monument was undercut in stages, shored up, and buttressed with stone blocks cemented together.

Meanwhile, many suggestions came into the society for less costly designs than Mills's. Boston designer M. P. Hapgood said the Washington Monument should be a cathedral-like tower with an angel standing on the uppermost spire. Somebody in California proposed an elaborate monument that, by today's standards, resembled a cross between the Statue of Liberty and the top of the Empire State Building. It fell to an attorney, not an architect, to come up with the best suggestion of all.

George Perkins Marsh, the U.S. Minister to Italy, had been fascinated by the obelisks of Egypt and had sketched many of them. Throw out Mills's pantheon and all the other gingerbread, said Marsh. Preserve only the obelisk. Marsh pointed out that the proportions of the best-known Egyptian obelisks were almost precisely ten times the base dimension. The Washington Monument shaft was 55 feet square at its baseline. Therefore, the monument should rise to about 550 feet, not 600, as in Mills's design.

"There will no doubt be people who will be foolish enough to insist on a peephole somewhere," said Marsh. "If they must be gratified, the window should be of the exact form and size of one of the stones." The society liked Marsh's plan. Best of all, the monument could be built at a more realistic cost.

The Corps of Engineers found that the monument had settled four inches—two and a half inches during the sixteen-month foundation-rebuilding job. They bored a narrow shaft 150 feet from the foundation and built a model of the monument, which was placed in the hole. The small shaft is checked annually to determine further settling, which has been negligible. Colonel Casey found that settling had twisted the shaft nearly one and a half inches toward the northwest. The monument was therefore out of alignment with the desired north-south, east-west planes. Workers would have to twist the shaft back again. The job was done by adjusting the placements of the upper slabs of marble so that the upper faces would line up with the chief points of the compass.

On a breezy Saturday, August 7, 1880, more than thirty years after the cornerstone was laid, the 26 feet of Know-Nothings' marble was removed. The first of the new slabs was lifted by a steam-powered hoist to the 150-foot level scaffolding, where President and Mrs. Rutherford B. Hayes and their party were waiting. Wet mortar was smeared at the northeast corner. Into the cement President Hayes pressed a coin inscribed with his initials, the month, day, and year. Others in the presidential party placed similar coins, and the hoist lowered the new marble into place.

Up to the 150-foot level, the marble had been laid with a backing of broken stones. From that point to the 452-foot level, the marble would be backed with New England granite, and the remaining eight feet with through-and-through marble slabs. Because Maryland marble was temporarily unavailable, 26 feet of Massachusetts marble was laid. Artisans believed they had achieved a perfect color match, but the Massachusetts marble weathered to a different hue. The result came to be called "Washington's Ring," and it can easily be seen today.

Steam-engine hoists chuffed, cables whined, and the marble slabs were raised to the lofty heights. From there, derricks lifted the blocks into place. Workers on the scaffolding were constantly endangered by strong winds swirling around the monument. Soon after the Corps of Engineers took over construction, a life net was rigged around the monument just under the scaffolding. The total work force was never large, but there were several falls. The net saved them all.

A pyramid-shaped capstone, 55 feet high and consisting of 262 marble stones, was built as the shaft neared the 500-foot level. At the same time, a solid aluminum casting was made to crown the capstone. The block was just under nine inches high and weighed one hundred ounces. With aluminum selling at $1.10 an ounce, the capstone was the largest and the costliest block of aluminum cast up to that time. Three of the block's faces were inscribed with the names and memorable dates of the monument's progress. On the fourth side was inscribed "Laus Deo," meaning Praise to God. Nowhere on the block was Washington's name mentioned.

The $110 block was displayed in the window of Tiffany's jewelry store in New York City. Later, when it was shown in other cities, schoolchildren lined up to step over it so they could say they had "walked over the tallest building in the world." For a time the monument was the world's tallest structure, and until 1965 was the tallest monument in the world. In that year, the 630-foot stainless steel St. Louis Gateway Arch, part of the Jefferson National Expansion Memorial, was completed.

On August 9, 1884, the Corps of Engineers laid the last of their 9,613 marble slabs. On Saturday, December 6, a stormy day with intermittent rain and high, cold wind howling around the 500-foot-level scaffolding, the 3,300-pound capstone and aluminum crown were gingerly hoisted up through the inside of the shaft and raised to

Putting the finishing touches on the Washington Monument capstone.

Lifting the capstone into place, December 6, 1884.

the top by a system of ropes and pulleys. After the capstone was cemented in place, an American flag was unfurled from the peak, and an artillery salute reverberated throughout the capital.

At last the monument was virtually complete. It stands 555 feet 5 1/8 inches. The monument weighs 81,120 tons and cost $1,187,710.31. Thirty-mile-an-hour winds buffeting the monument cause it to sway no more than .125 inch. It is said to be able to withstand 145-mile-an-hour gales.

The monument was dedicated by President Chester A. Arthur on the day before Washington's Birthday, 1885. That night a mighty fireworks show lit up the monument. The grand finale depicted Washington on horseback as five hundred silver skyrockets exploded. Fireworks became an annual Fourth of July tradition at the monument. The Washington National Monument was opened to the public October 9, 1888, when the elevator and fifty flights of stairs (898 steps) were completed and the memorial stones laid in the interior walls. Today, the elevator ride up takes seventy seconds; it comes down in sixty.

Inscribed stones came from forty states, nineteen cities, the Cherokee nation, and ten foreign countries. Greece sent a block of white marble from the Parthenon. There is lava from Vesuvius, a stone from the Alexandria Library in Egypt, and one from Napoleon's tomb in St. Helena. Other memorials came from Masonic lodges, other fraternal groups, the Oldest Inhabitants Association, and seven temperance organizations. Baltimore schoolchildren and teachers in the Buffalo public schools sent stones. The New York and the Philadelphia fire departments gave memorials, as did Invincible Fire Company Number Five of Cincinnati. So, too, did "Americans living in Foo-Chow, China, 1857," during the heydey of clipper ships. Hawaii sent a stone in 1936 to bring the total to 190.

Hardly a year passes that something or someone doesn't make headlines at the monument. People have tried to walk down the 898 steps on their hands. Couples have tried—unsuccessfully—to get married in the observation gallery. Blackstone the Magician's request to make a horse disappear from the observation tower also was turned down. There have been many baseball-throwing stunts from the eight gallery windows. On August 29, 1892, a ball was caught by "Gabby" Street, a catcher for the Washington team. Musicians have tested their voice projections from the tower. In 1915 Alfred Warsaw,

The Washington National Monument is the tallest all-masonry structure in the world.

a Metropolitan Opera baritone, squirmed through one of the windows. While two volunteers held his waist and legs, he sang the first two verses of a ballad, "Answer." He won a twenty-dollar-goldpiece bet when fellow musicians heard him as they stood on the street below.

Perhaps the most bizarre happenstance was that which sometimes occurred with weather changes, especially after a rainfall. The interior walls of the monument reacted slowly to the weather; moisture condensed in the upper air within the shaft. With water seepage through the mortar and the pores of the stones, the result was a sprinkling of rain. The rain inside the Washington Monument forced U.S. Park Service attendants who escorted visitors to put on galoshes and raincoats. Installation of a dehumidifier and better weatherproofing of the exterior walls solved the problem. Still, weather makes the monument do strange things. On sunny days the monument becomes a sundial. At 12:30 p.m., the shadow cast by the shaft points toward the White House.

But headline hunters and demonstrators of every stripe fail to deter the more than two million people who annually visit the monument. From the observatory they marvel at the panoramic view of the capital, including the White House to the north, the Jefferson Memorial to the south, the Capitol Building to the east, and the Lincoln Memorial to the west. If the view is unexcelled, so too was the tribute by a fourteen-year-old Washington, D.C., youth. His name is long forgotten, but he perhaps wrote the most fitting testimonial of all to the Washington National Monument: "It looks like a giant's spike God might have driven into the earth and said: 'Here I stake a claim for the home of liberty.' "

V

Old Ironsides

BULLIES BEGAN ATTACKING the United States only two years after it won independence. Resenting competition from American ships which were building trade in European and Pacific markets, Great Britain and France seized United States merchantmen and forced their crews to join their navies. England and France were at war. Defenseless American ships provided a ready source of crewmen for their undermanned fleets. Moreover, in the Mediterranean, Barbary pirates captured eleven United States ships and demanded ransom for their more than one hundred officers and crew.

The United States had fought for freedom on land. By 1794 Congress realized the young nation must fight again to win freedom on the high seas. But with what? There was no navy. It had been disbanded after the Revolution, and all ships had been sold. On March 27, 1794, Congress created the United States Navy and voted to build six frigates, including one to be named the *Constitution*, "for the great bulwark of our government." The others were the *President*, the *United States*, the *Constellation*, the *Congress*, and the *Chesapeake*.

There were many reasons for choosing frigates over the two other main classes of warships, corvettes and ships-of-the-line. Corvettes were small, mounting only around 20 guns. Although ships-of-the-line had upward of 110-120, they lacked the speed and maneuverability of frigates, which were an in-between size. Frigates were ideally suited for going after the Barbary pirates, who presented the most immediate threat. The speedy three-masted cruisers han-

Stern view of Old Ironsides *in drydock, 1964.*

dled well in all types of weather and packed a powerful punch, 30 or more guns. The top or spar deck carried cannon, and so did the gun deck below it.

Under the gun deck was the berth deck, where the crew of around four hundred slept. A large crew was an important consideration if landing assaults became necessary against Barbary forts. Below the berth deck was the orlop for storage. Plenty of storage space enabled frigates to cruise for months without returning to port for supplies, an essential quality because of the distance they would travel to the Mediterranean.

Still another plus was the threat of eventual war with England or France. Six American frigates could in no way stand up to Britain's fleet of more than six hundred, including a hundred frigates. France's navy was similarly overpowering. If war came, the frigates would be best qualified for capturing enemy merchant ships carrying war materiel and other supplies which would be needed by the United States. If frigates encountered a ship-of-the-line or an enemy squadron, they could hit fast and hard and have a good chance of escaping without being sunk or captured.

President George Washington put War Secretary Henry Knox in charge of the project. The fact that America had never built a warship of this size, much less six of them at one time, did not seem to worry anybody. Knox assembled a design team headed by Joshua Humphreys, forty-two, a Philadelphia shipbuilder. Assisting him was Josiah Fox, thirty-one, a brilliant naval designer. Humphreys and Fox were Quakers, a religious group opposing war. When the Quakers learned what Humphreys and Fox were doing, the two were expelled, although it is believed that Humphreys was later reinstated. Fox said the Philadelphia Quakers who ousted him had no authority because he was not a member of their group. Working closely with Humphreys and Fox was William Doughty, a master shipbuilder and draftsman, and the office manager of Humphreys's yard.

Their innovative design for a heavier, speedier, and larger than normal frigate mounting more guns was to revolutionize naval construction. The six frigates varied slightly in design. The *Constitution* would be 204 feet long, tapering to 175 feet at the waterline, and $43\frac{1}{2}$ feet in beam, or width. Length made the frigate about the size of a small ship-of-the-line. The width was about 5 feet more than standard frigates. The extra width provided a better angle for securing the rigging ropes that steadied the masts. Too, the added beam gave greater stability in high seas. The result enabled designers to plan for more and heavier than usual armament that would have greater stability in high seas.

The *Constitution*'s masts varied in size over the years. Today her foremast stands 198 feet, the mainmast 220, and the mizzenmast 172½. The design called for thicker than normal masts. The *Constitution*'s main, 53½ inches thick at the bottom, ensured greater strength if rigging or parts of the mast were cut in battle. Not only were the masts more stoutly built, but so was the hull framing and planking.

The gun deck of Old Ironsides *held thirty-eight long guns, nineteen on each broadside battery. Photo shows the port side.*

In some places the hull was to be 21 inches thick, a feature which would give the *Constitution* her nickname. The *Constitution* would do 13½ knots.

Still another innovation was the mounting of gun-deck ports about eight feet above the waterline. Traditional mountings called for placement of guns closer to the waterline to prevent ships from becoming top-heavy. The higher position, however, would provide the *Constitution* with a distinct fighting advantage in rough weather. During storms, other ships were forced to close their lower gunports to avoid taking on water.

The *Constitution* would have greater firepower, too. Two types of cast-iron cannons—long guns and stubby carronades—were common at this time. The longs, sometimes called Long Toms, measured 9¼ and 10½ feet long and were mounted on four-wheel carriages. They had a maximum effective range of about 1,200 yards. Each weighed between 6,300 and 6,800 pounds and was operated by a nine- to fourteen-man gun crew. They fired a 24-pound ball. Heavier shots, tradition held, resulted in a dangerous recoil that could snap rope restraints. Rolling across the deck, the guns could punch holes in the sides of the ship. The *Constitution*'s designers believed that the wider, sturdier ship could safely handle 24-pound shot.

Carronades were about four feet long and were mounted on casters. They were lethal during close-range firing at targets of up to four hundred yards distance. Carronades had several advantages over Long Toms. They were lighter, weighing just over a ton, and could safely be mounted on the top deck. The longs required two to three minutes for loading and firing. Carronades needed but one. The carronades' four- to nine-man gun crews could fire a heavier thirty-two-pound shot which was extremely effective for smashing holes in enemy hulls.

Although designed for forty-four guns, the *Constitution* mounted fifty-five at the start of the War of 1812. There were twenty-five guns, mostly carronades, on the top deck, and thirty of the Long Tom type on the gun deck below. The guns gave the *Constitution* the capability of firing a mighty broadside of between 700 and 750 pounds of shot.

The *Constitution* was to displace 2,200 tons and sit slightly more than twenty feet in the water. The captain's quarters were at the extreme rear, or aft. Officers had staterooms. Crewmen slung hammocks on the gun and berth decks. The ship carried 54,000 gallons of water and 8,000 gallons of rum, which was rationed daily to crewmen. There was storage space for six months of provisions for a crew of 475.

There were many construction hurdles. First of all, there were no navy yards for building the ships. What was more, Secretary Knox told Congress, the wood for the ships was still standing somewhere in forests; the iron for the cannon was still in the form of ore in the mines, and the seed for the flax sails and hemp rope rigging had yet to be planted. Compounding problems was Humphreys's insistence on extensive use of a scarce wood, live oak, for the framework. Live oak, he explained, was stronger and more durable than other types of wood.

The navy yard problem was easy. Contracts were let to commercial shipyards in Philadelphia, New York, Baltimore, Norfolk, and Portsmouth, New Hampshire. The order for the *Constitution* went to a Boston shipyard operated by three brothers, Edward, Edmund, and Joseph Hartt. Army Colonel George Claghorne was named naval constructor. Congress decided that the frigates' captains should supervise construction. Samuel Nicholson was appointed skipper of the ship that did not exist. Congress also voted to stop construction if negotiations for peace with the Barbary pirates became successful.

The stew of commercial shipbuilders, army and naval officers, each with their pet ideas, resulted in construction by committee, an arrangement that created more problems. Claghorne and Nicholson argued frequently. On one occasion Nicholson lashed out at Claghorne with his cane. Yard workers separated them. Nor was Nicholson a hero to the workers. He announced he was reserving for himself the honor of being the first to hoist the flag over the *Constitution*. But Samuel Bentley, a yard worker, waited until Nicholson left the ship, then proceeded to run up the flag.

Live oak was found on four islands off Georgia. There was enough of it on three of them, Blythe, Glover and Blackbeard, to build all the frigates. The government bought the islands for $16,000. White oak for parts of the *Constitution*'s hull came from Abington, south of Boston, and from the Kennebec Valley in Maine. Wood for the keel came from New Jersey. Pine for her masts was felled near Unity, Maine. The logs were dragged to tidewater at the Sheepscot River

Main or spar deck of Old Ironsides *looking from the stern toward the bow.*

and towed by ship to Boston. The yellow pine for her decks came from South Carolina and Georgia.

The *Constitution* required nearly 43,000 square feet of linen for thirty-six sails, which were fashioned in the loft of Boston's old Granary Building, where Park Street Church stands today. The more than two miles of hemp rigging was made by Cordwainers, Boston. Anchors were forged by a Mr. Barstow at Hanover, Massachusetts. Carvings, ornamental fittings, and the bow figurehead of Hercules holding a club and scroll representing the written Constitution were done by Skillings Brothers, Boston.

Soon after the *Constitution*'s keel was laid, a letter came to Secretary Knox. It was signed by a Boston coppersmith, Paul Revere, who said he could supply copper bolts and other parts "as cheap as anyone." Revere said he had a secret forging process. The price would be $3,820.33. He got the job.

Gradually the frigate took shape while adz-swinging workers chiseled the timbers to form pieces of the framework and hull. (An adz is a pick-shaped cutting tool with a thin, curved blade.) It was not a mass-production job; each piece of the hull was individually formed. The timbers were joined in many places with treenails (pronounced "trunnels") of locust wood. When the sea dampened the treenails, they would expand to form a solid weld. The hull below the waterline was covered with a protective layer of copper sheathing provided by Revere.

Then came news that the Barbary pirate problem had been solved by a new treaty. All work on the frigates stopped. The story of how they built the *Constitution* might have ended here except that England and France were becoming bolder in their attacks on American shipping. Congress voted money to complete the *Constitution, Constellation,* and *United States.* Eventually, the other three frigates were finished, too.

The *Constitution,* built at a cost of $302,718, was scheduled for launching September 20, 1797. Boston was in a holiday mood. Claghorne cautioned the large crowd of spectators to stand well back to avoid a drenching from the mighty wave when the *Constitution* splashed into the water. Workmen sledgehammered away the blocks holding the ship in the cradle. She did not move. Screws were applied to nudge the bulky frigate off the ways. The *Constitution* moved but twenty-seven feet. The tide ran out, and Claghorne gave up. Two days later a second attempt failed, and there were mutterings that the *Constitution* would likely become a jinxed ship. A suitable tide would not occur again until October 21, a Saturday.

By noon that day a crowd of several thousand had gathered. Captain James Sever, skipper of the frigate *Congress,* broke a bottle of Madeira wine against the *Constitution*'s bow. A Boston newspaper reported, "At 15 minutes after 12, at the first stroke of the spur shores, she commenced a movement into the water with such steadiness, majesty and exactness as to fill almost every breast with sensations of joy and delight." The crowd cheered and cannons boomed.

When the Barbary pirates broke the peace, the *Constitution* headed for the Mediterranean, where it joined in combined land and sea actions. Her hull and masts took some shots, and the Hercules

Worker makes a new mast for Old Ironsides.

figurehead was lost in a collision with another ship in September 1804. The pirates surrendered, and a peace treaty was drafted aboard the *Constitution* on June 3, 1805. The Barbary pirate threat was over.

Seven years later, June 18, 1812, the United States declared war against England. Despite Britain's continuing contempt for America's right to freedom on the high seas and the impressment of more than six thousand sailors into the English Navy, most historians believe that negotiations then in progress could have avoided war. The declaration barely squeaked through Congress. The war was as unpopular as it was rash. From a naval standpoint, it was suicidal.

America's fleet consisted of six frigates and about fourteen smaller ships. The British Royal Navy, known the world over as "The Colossus of the Seven Seas," was still glorying in Admiral Horatio Nelson's devastating defeat of the combined French and Spanish fleets at the Battle of Trafalgar, October 21, 1805. Since then, the British Navy had not lost a single fight. British naval officers and architects jeered the *Constitution* and the other "fir-built frigates," and said their clumsy design made them too sluggish for rapid maneuvering and effective fighting. President James Madison was considering his Cabinet's suggestion that the Navy sit out the war in port to avoid capture or destruction. The *Constitution*'s brash captain, Isaac Hull, thirty-seven, had other ideas. Without waiting for President Madison's decision, he put out to sea to escape the inevitable British blockade of American ports.

On the afternoon of August 19, 1812, the *Constitution* was cruising in rough seas six hundred miles east of Boston when the lookout sighted the forty-nine-gun British frigate *Guerrière*. The ships and their captains were no strangers. A month earlier, off Atlantic City, New Jersey, Hull had accidentally found himself in the midst of the *Guerrière* and four other warships. There was no way the *Constitution* could have survived against these odds, and Hull had managed to escape. Before the war, the *Guerrière*'s captain, cocky twenty-eight-year-old James R. Dacres, had met Hull and boasted he could whip any American frigate. Hull accepted the challenge. To the winner would go a hat.

The *Constitution* broke out all sails to intercept the *Guerrière*. Dacres was as eager for battle as Hull, and he fired first. The ball splintered the *Constitution*'s rail. Hull leaped up to get a better view and ripped open the seat of his trousers. The British drew first blood as more

The USS Constitution *in battle with the British ship* Guerrière.

Guerrière shots slammed home. A gunner fell dead beside his Long Tom. The *Constitution* handled as well as her builders intended. Hull held his fire while maneuvering to bring his starboard broadside to bear.

"We came up into the wind in gallant style," wrote Long Tom gunner Moses Smith. "The Stars and Stripes never floated more proudly than they did at that moment."

Hull called out the order: "Let every man look well to his aim . . . now pour it into them!" The *Constitution*'s Long Toms and carronades thundered a broadside that shook the ship. When the smoke cleared, Hull saw that the broadside had sliced off the *Guerrière*'s mizzenmast and caused other severe damage.

Dacres was in trouble. He ordered his gunners to shoot to poke holes in the *Constitution*'s hull. The *Guerrière*'s broadsides thudded against the *Constitution,* but caused only slight damage. Dacres ordered heavier cannonballs. One of the largest slammed into the *Constitution*'s hull, bounced off and plunked into the sea. The *Constitution*'s crew cheered. Somebody, nobody knows who, said, "Her sides are made of iron!" And that is how *Old Ironsides* was born.

The two frigates whaled at each other for the better part of an hour. Much of *Old Ironsides'* rigging was cut and some of her sails were ripped, but her stout masts held, and her hull continued to shake off the fearsome pounding by the *Guerrière*. *Old Ironsides'* quick maneuverability enabled Hull to come across the *Guerrière*'s bow and to fire a deadly storm of shot the length of her deck. The *Guerrière*'s fore and main masts toppled overboard. Dacres realized his hopeless situation and surrendered. The *Guerrière* suffered seventy-eight killed and wounded; *Old Ironsides* had fourteen casualties.

Dacres offered Hull his sword in the traditional token of surrender. Hull refused it. "I will not take a sword from one who knows so well how to use it. But I will trouble you for that hat." The story may be apocryphal, but it is known that Dacres became Hull's lifelong friend.

News of the victory could not have come at a better time. The war was going badly for the United States. England realized the symbolic value of the *Constitution*'s triumph. The *London Times* said, "He must be a weak politician who does not see how important this first triumph is in giving a tone and character to the war."

Old Ironsides was soon in action again, this time with Commodore

William Bainbridge in command. On December 29, 1812, off Brazil, the *Constitution* shattered the frigate *Java* in a two-hour battle that was a bloodier repetition of the encounter with the *Guerrière*. The battles, four months apart, coupled with the frigate *United States'* capture of the *Macedonian,* caused the British Admiralty to order its frigates to avoid action with the Americans. Naval architects in England immediately began copying the American design.

On the moonlit night of February 20, 1815, *Old Ironsides* made short work of the frigate *Cyane* and the sloop *Levant.* The battle occurred three days after the United States and Great Britain had signed a peace treaty, but word had not reached the captains. *Old Ironsides* was the naval heroine of the war. She inflicted more damage on the British than any other American warship. To this day, *Old Ironsides* symbolizes the United States' victorious claim to freedom on the high seas.

But war heroes are sometimes soon forgotten. Seventeen years later, *Old Ironsides* lay rotting at her Boston Navy Yard berth. A naval commission recommended that she be broken up and sold for scrap. Oliver Wendell Holmes, then twenty-one, a recent graduate of Harvard University, read of the proposed junking. On a piece of scrap paper he wrote a poem and sent it to the Boston *Advertiser,* which published it on September 16, 1830:

Old Ironsides

Ay, tear her tattered ensign down!
   Long has it waved on high,
And many an eye has danced to see
   That banner in the sky;
Beneath it rung the battle shout,
   And burst the cannon's roar;—
The meteor of the ocean air
   Shall sweep the clouds no more!

Her deck, once red with heroes' blood,
   Where knelt the vanquished foe,
When winds were hurrying o'er the flood,
   And waves were white below,
No more shall feel the victor's tread,
   Or know the conquered knee;—

> The harpies of the shore shall pluck
> The eagle of the sea!
>
> Oh, better that her shattered hulk
> Should sink beneath the wave;
> Her thunders shook the mighty deep
> And there should be her grave;
> Nail to the mast her holy flag,
> Set every threadbare sail,
> And give her to the god of storms,
> The lightning and the gale!

Reprinted throughout the United States, the poem sparked massive public protests against the junking. Hundreds of letters poured in to Congressmen. The Navy changed its mind, and Congress voted money to make *Old Ironsides* shipshape. With Hull again in command for the occasion, the *Constitution* entered a Boston Navy Yard drydock. The first careful examination of the hull since launching showed that it was badly out of line. The bowing was caused when she stuck fast on the ways during launching, and by her heavy guns.

While Naval Constructor Josiah Barker supervised the hull-straightening, a skilled Boston woodcarver, Laban S. Beecher, was commissioned by Captain Jesse D. Elliott, Naval Yard Commander, to make a life-sized figurehead of President Andrew Jackson. The idea brewed a political storm. A group of Boston Whigs threatened to tar and feather Elliott, and Beecher, too. The louder they protested, the more stubborn Elliott became. The figurehead was mounted on the *Constitution*.

The Jackson figurehead in concept was angering. The Jackson figurehead in place was inflaming. After new threats, Captain Elliott ordered two ships-of-the-line to berth alongside *Old Ironsides*. A twenty-four-hour Marine Corps guard was posted near her bow. Samuel Worthington Dewey, twenty-eight, a merchant sea captain with a reputation for practical jokes, overheard a countinghouse operator offer a one-hundred-dollar reward to anyone who cut off the figurehead.

Dewey seized his chance on the dark night of July 2, 1834, during a thunderstorm that scudded clouds over the moon. Rightly guessing that the sentry would expect trouble to come from shore, definitely not from sea on this stormy night, Dewey rowed to the Navy Yard

Rotting old hulk of USS Constitution *preparatory to 1927 reconstruction.*

and climbed aboard *Old Ironsides*. While the sentry's back was turned, Dewey sawed off Jackson's head, put it in a sack, and rowed away. At daybreak the sentry discovered the decapitation.

Dewey became the man of the Whigs' hour. Whether he ever collected the one hundred dollars is unknown. Jackson's head was the centerpiece at a Whig banquet. Dewey took the head to Washington and presented it to the flustered Navy Secretary. Captain Elliott was not amused; he ordered the head remounted.

Old Ironsides' last service as an active fighting ship was in 1852, when she hunted slave ships in the Mediterranean and caught the *N. H. Gambrill*. Berthed as a school ship at Annapolis when the Civil War started, she was removed to Newport, Rhode Island, far from the threat of Confederate capture. Her sister ship, the *United States*, was burned at Norfolk to prevent her capture by the rebels. *Old Ironsides* was the only frigate of the original six to survive in one piece. The *Chesapeake* had been captured by the British in 1813 and

Old Ironsides *was turned into an ugly barracks when a barnlike structure was added to top deck.*

destroyed; the *President* was taken off New York City in 1815 and scrapped; the *Congress* was junked at Norfolk in 1836; the *Constellation* was taken apart in 1854 and rebuilt as a twenty-gun corvette. She is today berthed in Baltimore but is no longer an officially commissioned ship.

After *Old Ironsides* hauled a load of trolley cars and locomotives to France for an exhibition, she was turned into a barracks. Her masts were removed, and a barnlike structure was built over her spar deck. *Old Ironsides* became an ugly old houseboat. In this sad condition she was towed to Boston for the hundredth anniversary of her launching. By then, *Old Ironsides* was a rotting hulk. A Navy tug kept her afloat by nightly pumping out the thousand gallons of water that seeped through her hull every day.

A naval board of inquiry decided in 1905 that *Old Ironsides* had outlived her usefulness; the board recommended she be towed to sea and used for target practice. Again the Navy badly underestimated public opinion. National reaction was similar to that following the publication of Holmes's poem. Congress voted $100,000 to rebuild her. In 1925 she was in bad shape again. Congress authorized a complete overhaul, but said the cost must largely be met by public donations. The result was one of the greatest outpourings of patriotism in the nation's history. Students across the country contributed pennies. Paramount Pictures made a movie which brought in more money. In all, about fifty million Americans gave more than $600,000, and Congress voted $300,000.

Old Ironsides went into drydock on June 16, 1927. Lieutenant John A. Lord, last of the Navy's wooden-ship builders, was in charge. He scoured New England for craftsmen skilled in shaping wood. Where to find live oak was a problem until someone recalled that 500,000 board feet of it had years before been stored underwater in Commodores Pond Naval Air Station, Pensacola, Florida. A search found it still there.

Other materials—wood, iron, and sailcloth—came from many states. Much of it was donated. The West Coast Lumbermen's Association gave five carloads of Douglas fir for masts and spars. The wood appropriately came from Bainbridge Island in Puget Sound, across from Seattle. Railroads hauled the lumber free. One of the timbers was 109 feet long and required two flatcars to carry it. As *Old Ironsides'* new masts were being seated, a five-dollar gold coin was placed under the foremast, a silver dollar under the main, and an old copper penny and other coins under the mizzen. The practice dated from antiquity: coins placed heads up under masts guaranteed the crew safe passage into eternity if the ship met with mishap.

On October 8, 1930, the new *Old Ironsides*—only ten percent of the original ship remained—was reintroduced to the public. Soon afterward, *Old Ironsides* left for a cruise from Maine to Washington to show Americans the result of their contributions. Ninety American cities were visited, and hundreds of thousands of people walked her decks. Returning to Boston in 1934, she took up permanent residence at the naval shipyard.

In April 1973 the Navy drydocked *Old Ironsides* for a three-year

Each year Old Ironsides *goes on a "turn around" cruise in Boston Harbor. The frigate is turned 130 degrees upon returning to its berth so that both sides will be exposed equally to the weather.*

refurbishing program costing more than $4 million. Her seventeen tons of three-sixteenths-inch copper hull sheathing was replaced. Part of the hull planking below the waterline was redone, and her masts, yards, and rigging were refinished. Much of *Old Ironsides'* top deck was replaced. Smelling of fresh lumber and paint, *Old Ironsides* returned to her berth to greet visitors during the celebration of America's Bicentennial. Commander Tyrone G. Martin, the fifty-third skipper of *Old Ironsides,* said, "She should be able to withstand another fifty years of service."

Our oldest fighting ship still in full commission, *Old Ironsides* is the flagship of the commandant of the First Naval District, an area including Maine, New Hampshire, Vermont, Massachusetts, and Rhode Island. Standing guard is a small crew of officers and men whose duties include the escort of group tours of students. Each year on Bunker Hill Day in mid-April, *Old Ironsides* leaves her berth for a brief cruise in Boston Harbor. She returns and docks on her opposite side, so that *Old Ironsides* is equally exposed to the weather.

Few recall the tribute paid *Old Ironsides* in 1927 by the Right Reverend Charles Slattery, Bishop of Massachusetts. His words are nevertheless as fresh and true today as *Old Ironsides'* paint and timbers: "The world is prone to judge our nation as commercial, interested only in the surging wealth which flows in upon our people. We do not consider our national treasures to be in the great modern buildings which tower in the sky. We find our treasures in Independence Hall in Philadelphia and in the good ship *Constitution,* which today takes on a new life and will become, we trust, an inspiration to our children and our children's children."

VI

The Statue of Liberty

SHORTLY AFTER President Abraham Lincoln was assassinated on April 14, 1865, some forty thousand French people contributed to a gold medal which was presented to Mrs. Lincoln. It bore the inscription: "Dedicated by French democracy to Lincoln . . . honest Lincoln who abolished slavery, reestablished the union, and saved the Republic, without veiling the Statue of Liberty." There was no Statue of Liberty in New York Harbor at the time, but the inscription was prophetic of what was to stand, twenty-one years later, as one of the world's masterworks of art and engineering.

Several months after Lincoln's death, a memorial to the long friendship between France and the United States was proposed at a dinner hosted in Versailles by Édouard de Laboulaye, a legal scholar who had written many interpretations of the American government. Among his guests were prominent men of letters, politics and the arts, including a thirty-one-year-old sculptor, Frédéric-Auguste Bartholdi, who specialized in patriotic statues. Laboulaye and his friends decided to commemorate Franco-American friendship with a colossal monument. Like the medal, it would be paid for by public donations and be a gift from the people of France to the citizens of the United States. The group agreed to send Bartholdi to America to come up with some ideas for the design as well as a site.

Bartholdi was not lacking in commissions, and it was not until 1871 that he was able to go. Arriving in New York Harbor, Bartholdi noted several islands, among them Bedloe's, site of the abandoned

Lights in the Statue of Liberty torch are 2,500 times brighter than full moonlight and can be seen far out to sea.

Fort Leonard Wood, named after a War of 1812 hero. It was at that moment, Bartholdi said later, that he conceived the idea of a statue, similar to one he had hoped to create as a lighthouse near the Mediterranean entrance to the new Suez Canal, which was completed by France in 1869.

Bartholdi envisioned the American statue as a robed goddess, a broken chain at her feet, freed from enslavement. Cradled in her left arm would be a law tablet inscribed July 4, 1776, in Roman numerals. Her right hand would hold high the torch of freedom. He would name his statue *Liberty Enlightening the World.* During his travels throughout the United States, Bartholdi kept an open mind for other ideas. In Washington, he studied the Capitol Building, but disliked the design of the dome almost as much as he found the still-unfinished Washington Monument too plain for his tastes. At the end of his stay, nothing had inspired him more than Bedloe's Island as the site for his *Liberty.*

Bartholdi returned to Paris and began transferring his concept into small plaster models. He had studied paintings of Liberty and American silver dollars with their versions of Liberty's face, but was dissatisfied with all of them. He at last modeled *Liberty*'s face after that of his mother. Bartholdi developed his ideas while a Parisian seamstress, Jeanne-Emilie Baheux de Puysieux, posed for him. They were later married. Bartholdi decided to build the statue of durable, lightweight copper after ruling out stone (because it was too heavy) and bronze (which was too expensive). Even at that, he miscalculated the cost of the statue, which eventually came to $250,000.

Bartholdi's sponsors were pleased with his final four-foot statuette completed in August 1875. Spurred by their desire to present *Liberty* as a birthday gift during the United States Centennial celebration of independence the following year, they formed the Franco-American Union to raise the necessary funds. Laboulaye headed it, and the members included many prominent Frenchmen. Donations quickly were received, and Bartholdi began work. In New York and Philadelphia, meanwhile, committees were formed to raise money for the enormous stone pedestal on which *Liberty* would stand.

Transforming a 4-foot statuette into a 151-foot copper lady was one of the marvels of the century. Nothing of this magnitude had ever been done. The work was begun in the dingy shops of Gaget, Gauthier & Co., 25 rue de Chazelles, Paris, where Bartholdi super-

Latticework of Liberty's *left hand holding law tablet.*

vised dozens of sculptors, modelers, carpenters, and coppersmiths. Using his statuette as a guide, they cast a series of steadily larger ones until they had a plaster statue standing thirty-six feet tall. The shop was too small to hold anything larger, so they dissected *Liberty* into sections which were similarly enlarged until the pieces were full-size. The job required about nine thousand measurements for each section to ensure an accurate reproduction of the original, as well as an exact fit when the pieces of the statue were assembled.

Carpenters built latticework molds into which plaster was poured. When it set, they made more wooden molds which precisely copied *Liberty's* every curve, indentation, and bulge. Now it was the coppersmiths' turn. Using sheets of three-thirty-second-inch-thick copper, they pressed them into the wooden molds and hammered them to fit *Liberty*'s contours. Finally, they backed the sheets with iron straps to provide rigidity.

The question of what would prevent this thin-skinned Amazon from falling over was an engineering problem. Bartholdi turned that job over to Gustave Eiffel, a prominent bridge-builder who fourteen

Wooden molds copied Liberty's *every curve, indentation and bulge. Coppersmiths then pressed thin sheets of copper into the molds and hammered them to fit* Liberty's *contours.*

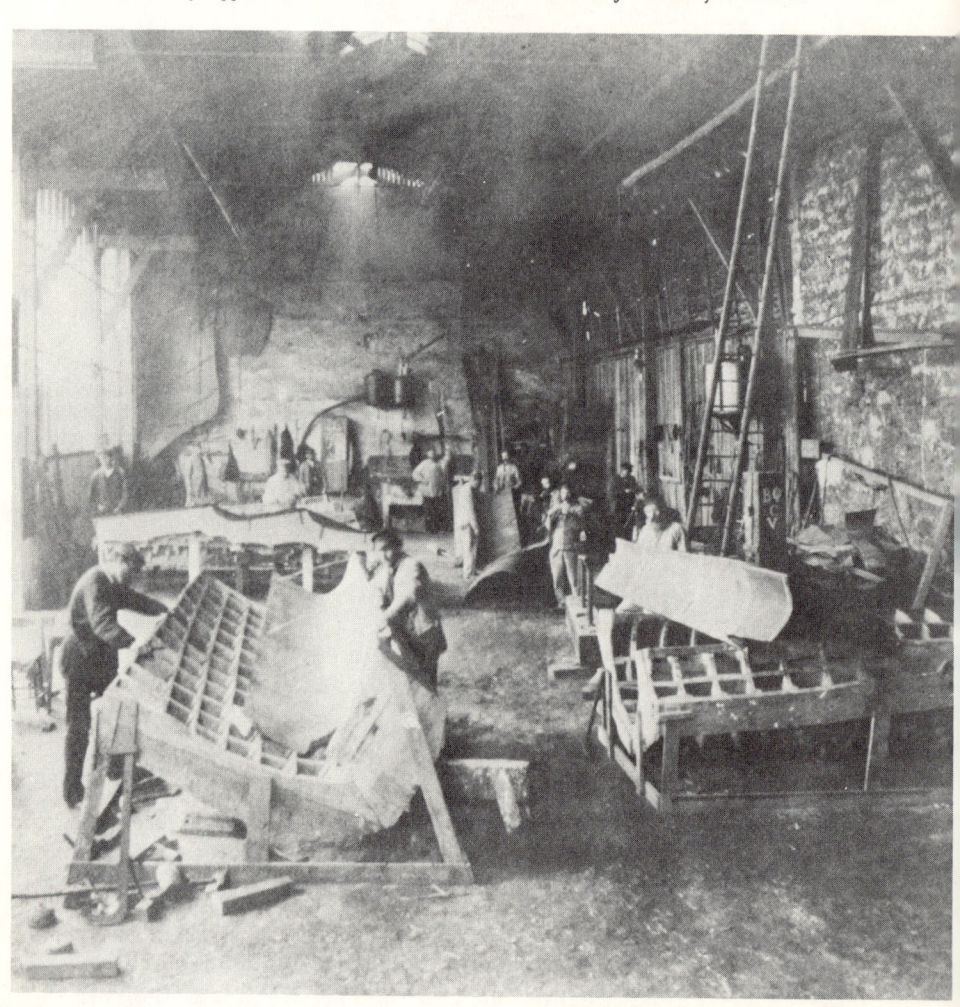

years later would erect the famous tower that bears his name. In the storage yard outside the Gaget, Gauthier workshop, Eiffel built a tall tower of four iron posts. Riveted to them was a skeleton framework of smaller beams, including a crisscrossing network of steel that formed the upraised arm. Eiffel designed the framework in such a way that each section of sheathing was independently supported and did not overlap those around it. As the copper sheets were completed, they were riveted at their back-bracing to the tower. When they were finished, the workers would use 200,000 pounds of copper to form more than three hundred sheets, plus 125 tons of steel for the framework.

By bits and pieces, *Liberty* took shape. The sheets were lifted by ropes up the side of the scaffolding surrounding Eiffel's tower and riveted in place. *Liberty*'s index finger was eight feet long; her nose four and a half feet. Her head, from ear to ear, measured ten feet, and her arm forty-two feet. The steadily rising statue intrigued Parisians who visited the crowded shops to look at the massive forms, the latticework and the molds; to smell the freshly cut lumber and the dank plaster; and to hear the incessant tap, tap, tap of carpenters' hammers and coppersmiths' mallets. Admission fees went into the statue-building fund, which was, as costs escalated, none too healthy.

In the United States, meanwhile, fund-raising for the pedestal was going badly. Work on it had not started, nor had the government approved the Bedloe's Island site. The public was mostly apathetic to the whole idea. Although there appeared to be little hope for a change in this attitude, Bartholdi seemed to be bothered not one bit by it when he came to the United States in 1876 as a member of the French delegation to the Centennial celebration.

The statue was not finished, else the United States would have found itself in the embarrassing position of having a statue on its hands and no place to put it. *Liberty*'s forearm and torch were done, however, and arrived in the United States for display at the Centennial Exposition in Philadelphia and later in New York City's Madison Square. In New York's Fourth of July parade, 1876, Bartholdi showed a large illustration of *Liberty* as she would look when finished. Later that day he went to Bedloe's Island to make some sketches. The ten-acre island derived its name from Isaack Bedloe, a Dutch merchant who had owned it in the late 1600s. Bedloe's Island was later

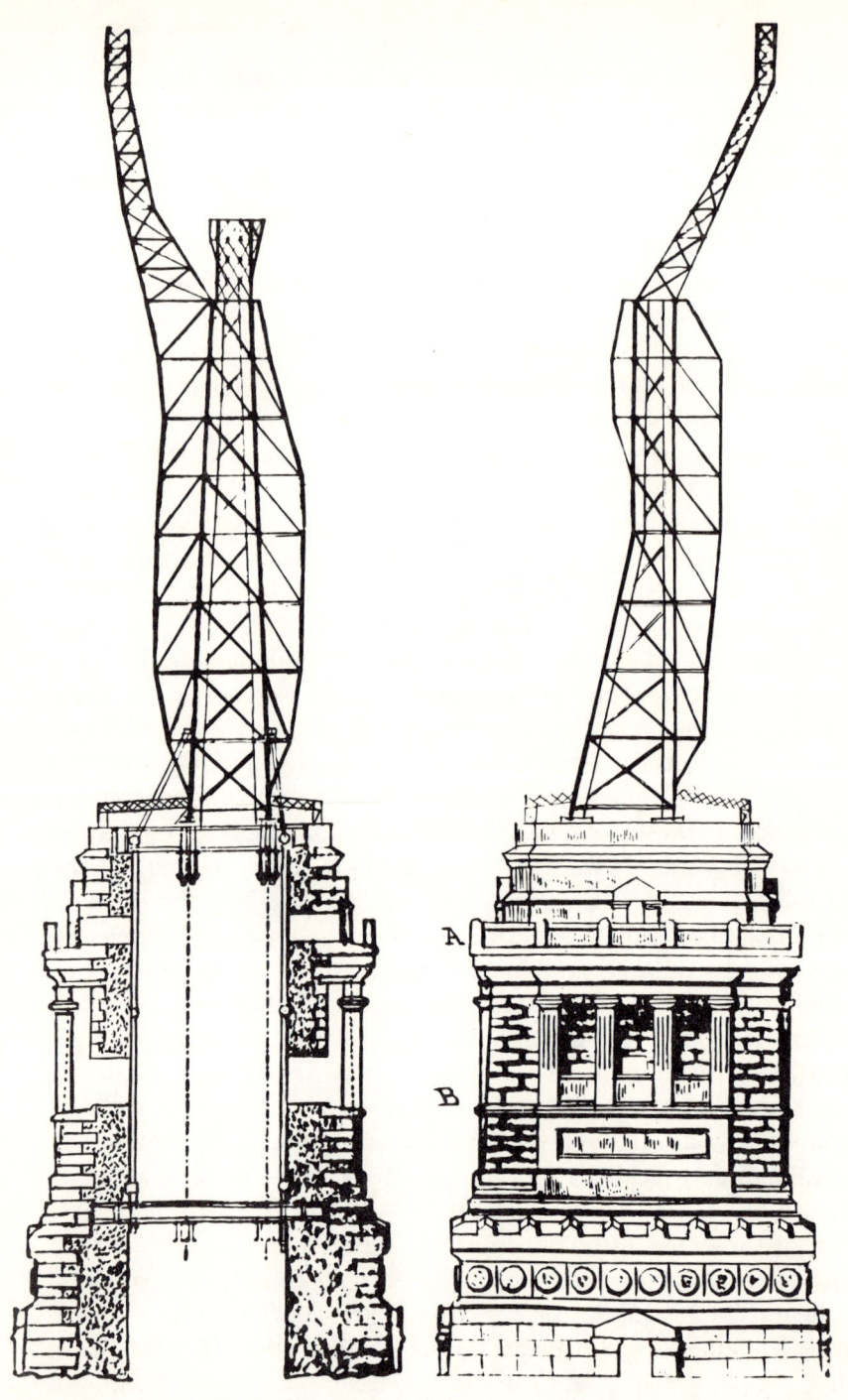

Framework of the statue, designed and executed by Gustave Eiffel. From Scientific American, *June 13, 1885.*

used as a quarantine station for immigrants, and in 1811 the star-shaped fort was completed. Bartholdi noted that the abandoned Fort Wood provided an ideal base for *Liberty*.

Bartholdi's visit and the sampling of the statue led to the formation, on January 2, 1877, of the American Committee on the Statue of Liberty. Through the efforts of these prominent lawyers, bankers and merchants, the Bedloe's Island site was approved, and fund-raising began anew.

Laboulaye and the Franco-American Union, meanwhile, renewed their campaign for public funds, and in 1878 *Liberty*'s head was exhibited at the Paris World's Fair. To further publicize the appeal, Bartholdi invited twenty newsmen to lunch on a platform built in *Liberty*'s kneecap. The cause was also helped as the shiny copper Statue of Liberty rose above nearby rooftops in December of that year and became a neighborhood curiosity. Lotteries and other fund-raisers were bringing in total donations of $250,000.

In this same year, Joseph Pulitzer came to New York from Missouri, where he had made a success of the St. Louis *Post-Dispatch*, and bought the faltering New York *World*. Pulitzer immediately seized upon the Statue of Liberty as a crusade and a circulation-builder. In a series of editorials, Pulitzer berated the wealthy for failing to fund the pedestal, and he began a campaign for nickels and dimes and pennies. Regardless of the amount of the contribution, contributors' names were printed in the *World*. But donations totaled only $135.75, and the campaign fizzled.

By then, the statue committee had raised $125,000. With this seed money, work on the foundation for the pedestal began on April 18, 1883. General Charles P. Stone was named construction engineer, and Richard M. Hunt, an architect who had worked with Thomas U. Walter on the building of the extensions to the Capitol Building in Washington, drew plans for the pedestal. It would be built of three-foot-thick blocks of granite from Leete's Island, Connecticut, set against three-foot layers of concrete. The pedestal would stand on a foundation of concrete down to the bedrock of Bedloe's Island.

Construction difficulties were almost instantly encountered, and resulted in delays and skyrocketing costs. Fort Wood was better built than the old drawings indicated. Digging down to bedrock required a force of fifty workers who hacked and blasted through thick masses

Framework of the statue nearing completion, 1886.

of stone and concrete. Cisterns and cells not shown on the plans were discovered and had to be sledgehammered. At last, a hole around a hundred feet square was opened, and workers began laying the foundation. Cement and other materials were ferried to Bedloe's Island aboard the *Bartholdi*. Gravel came from Weehawken, New Jersey, and sand from Staten Island. Tons of coal found in the old fort fueled the steam-powered cement mixers.

By July 1883 only two-thirds of the foundation was done, and the project was in deep financial trouble. Fund-raising schemes of every sort were tried, but only several thousand dollars was raised as autographs of Bartholdi were peddled and six-inch bronze statuettes of *Liberty* were sold for a dollar apiece. Artists, writers, and poets were asked to donate their work for auctioning. Among them was Emma Lazarus, a New York poet, who at first refused, then reconsidered. Five lines from her sonnet, "The New Colossus," written in 1883, would one day become almost as famous as the Statue of Liberty, and certainly synonymous with the statue's symbolic meaning:

> Give me your tired, your poor,
> Your huddled masses yearning to breathe free,
> The wretched refuse of your teeming shore,
> Send these, the homeless, tempest-tost to me,
> I lift my lamp beside the golden door!

The Lazarus poem went virtually ignored. Despite all efforts, the attitude of the American public was at best mostly ambivalent. Barring a miracle, there was little hope that *Liberty Enlightening the World* would ever stand in America.

There was, moreover, considerable opposition to the project. Some clergymen said that the United States needed no pagan goddess standing off its shore. Artists chipped at the statue's design, and one, his name long forgotten, said *Liberty*'s robe made her look like a sack of potatoes with a stick stuck in the top. *The New York Times* said the city could do very well indeed without a Statue of Liberty at the entrance to the city's harbor. If New York was not interested, other cities were. Boston, Chicago, Cleveland, Minneapolis, Philadelphia, St. Louis, and other cities indicated that they would build the pedestal if given the statue. There is evidence that a delegation went to Paris to persuade the Franco-American Union to give *Liberty* to Baltimore.

Eiffel's tower in storage yard at Gaget, Gauthier Cie, Paris. Note Liberty's *completed head standing left foreground.*

In 1884 Bartholdi finished his colossus. The copper lady gleaming in the sunlight stood as the tallest structure in Paris. *Liberty* was ready to be given to the United States. Tactful diplomacy among the French and Americans in Paris conveniently overlooked the fact that America was not ready for *Liberty,* but the formal presentation went ahead anyway on the Fourth of July, 1884, when United States Minister Levi P. Morton accepted it.

At the end of the year, *Liberty* still stood, tarnishing from the elements, in Gaget, Gauthier's cluttered storage yard. Work on the pedestal had by then stopped, and Chief Engineer Stone reported that there was only $2,866.89 in the building fund. An additional $100,000 was needed to complete the pedestal. And at that, they would have to postpone the installation of an elevator to take visitors to *Liberty's* observation tower.

Pulitzer was outraged. Editorials again picked up *Liberty's* cause as the publisher raged at rich and poor alike. "Who will save us from this National Disgrace?" he thundered. On March 16, 1885, the *World* resumed its fund-raising campaign. By now, its circulation had grown to around 230,000, and the newspaper had become one of New York's most influential.

Money trickled in at first, then grew to a steady flow as the *World* daily tallied the rising amount. Pennies came from orphans and schoolchildren. Churches took special collections. Workers contributed their lunch money. Thomas Alva Edison, William Waldorf Astor, John Pierpont Morgan, and other prominent citizens gave freely. The crusade was picked up by newspapers throughout the United States. Money poured in from as far away as California. The *World* daily reported the circumstances of the donations, although cynics suggested that reporters fabricated some of the stories. After former President Ulysses S. Grant died in July 1885, ten readers said they walked home from the funeral services so that they could each contribute their fifty-cent carfare to the fund. Encouraged by public response to the *World's* campaign, the statue committee ordered construction work resumed on the pedestal.

In Paris, meanwhile, *Liberty* was being disassembled. Each part was tagged for identification when it reached Bedloe's Island. Carpenters built crates for the parts. *Liberty's* left ear, pieces of her hair, a curl, the crown of her scalp, required a ten- by twenty-foot crate. Another held her nose, eyes, and three-foot-wide mouth. Accounts

Liberty's *head on display at Paris World's Fair, 1878.*

disagree over the number of crates required for the copper sheets and iron framework, but there were more than two hundred of them. Each box weighed between 150 pounds and three tons. The crates were trucked to a Paris railway station and lifted onto a seventy-car train which hauled them to Rouen for loading aboard the French warship *Isère*.

The *Isère* left late in May. Her arrival in New York on June 17, 1885, was greeted by the French North Atlantic Squadron, which escorted her into the harbor. A massive public welcome and parade followed two days later as the *World* reported that the fund had surpassed $75,000. At the warship's anchorage near Bedloe's Island, cranes lifted the crates from the *Isère* and set them gently onto lighters which took them to the island dock. There they were lifted onto a rail car and taken to storage sheds.

On August 11 the *World* headlined that the $100,000 goal had been reached. Work on the pedestal accelerated. To make certain that not even hurricane winds could topple the statue, four huge girders were formed into a square and set inside the twenty-nine-foot level of the 28,000-ton pedestal. A similar set of girders was erected a few feet from the top. The two sets were joined by iron tie beams which continued above the eighty-nine-foot-tall pedestal for attachment to Eiffel's framework. The pedestal was completed on April 22, 1886, when General Stone supervised the lifting of a two-ton block of granite into position. Workers smeared mortar, then showered silver coins into it as the derrick settled the block into place.

Eiffel's framework was attached to the pedestal, and Bartholdi began unpacking his copper sheets. On July 12, 1886, the first sheet, inscribed to Bartholdi, was riveted to the framework. The second sheet was dedicated to Pulitzer. The ocean crossing had been rough, and many of the sheets had to be reworked before being lifted into place by steam-powered hoists. In the haste to take the statue apart and get it to America, many pieces were incorrectly labeled. By trial and error, the sheets were lifted up and down until the correct one was found and riveted. There are varying accounts of the number of rivets used, but there were between 300,000 and 600,000 of them.

As *Liberty* took shape, there was no lack of news photographers, who found it easy to persuade many of the seventy-five workers, who looked like flies as they hung suspended from seats and planks, to sit on *Liberty*'s thumb or to stand beside a lock of her hair. On October

Forearm and torch on display at Philadelphia Centennial Exposition, 1876.

23, 1886, the last sheets were riveted into place on the nine- by five-foot sole of *Liberty*'s right foot, which had been left open to provide easy access into the statue.

Five days later, Thursday, October 28, 1886, the Statue of Liberty was formally dedicated in a steady rainfall. Ceremonies began with General Stone, astride a black horse, leading a parade of twenty thousand down Fifth Avenue from Fifty-seventh Street. Ships formed a crescent around Bedloe's Island, which was all but shrouded in fog. Bartholdi, standing in the torch, tugged a rope which pulled away the French tricolor flag draped over *Liberty*'s face. In accepting the statue on behalf of the people of the United States, President Grover Cleveland said, "We will not forget that Liberty has here made her home; nor shall her chosen altar be neglected."

From her foundation to the tip of her torch, *Liberty* stood 305 feet, 1 inch. The statue weighed 225 tons. It would not be long before the elements caused the copper to take on the flat, bluish green patina we know today. In 1909 the first elevator was installed. Bedloe's Island was renamed Liberty Island in 1956, the same year in which plans were announced for the American Museum of Immigration, which was built in additions to the base of the statue. The museum was opened in 1972 and is dedicated to the millions of immigrants to America. Since 1933 the Statue of Liberty has been under the jurisdiction of the National Park Service.

Bartholdi had but one disappointment in his masterpiece. The electric lamp in *Liberty*'s torch did not shine as far out to sea as he had hoped; he died of tuberculosis in Paris, October 4, 1904, without knowing that the problem would be solved. Twelve years later, the copper sheeting in the torch was replaced by six hundred pieces of red-and-yellow-tinted cathedral glass to enhance the beauty of the lights in the torch, which were later replaced by 1,000-watt bulbs that are 2,500 times brighter than full moonlight. The man who redesigned the torch was another sculptor unafraid of heights or of colossal works of art. His name was John Gutzon de la Mothe Borglum, who in 1927 began work on the four faces on Mount Rushmore, South Dakota.

VII

The Faces on Mount Rushmore

THERE WERE GOOD REASONS why Gutzon Borglum should not have gone to South Dakota to discuss the idea of carving huge faces on a mountainside in the Black Hills. Although he was the only one in the United States who knew how to do it, Borglum had many commissions in 1924, including a Confederate memorial he was sculpting on Stone Mountain, near Atlanta.

Why should he take on another project, especially one in the six-thousand-square-mile mountain wilderness of Ponderosa pine trees whose dark color gave the Black Hills their name? Memorials are best located where as many people as possible can easily see them, as, for example, the Statue of Liberty and the Washington National Monument. Except for Rapid City, South Dakota, the Black Hills were sparsely populated gold-mining villages. There were no paved roads into the forest, and only a few trails. Nor had any money been raised for the faces.

There was an even more compelling reason why Borglum should have turned down the invitation from South Dakota's official historian, Doane Robinson, to visit the Black Hills and to study the idea. Borglum was too old—going on sixty, not exactly in his youthful prime—to go off into the wilderness to look for an appropriate mountain. Even if he found one, the job would be a severe test of his strength. And when would he ever find the time to do it?

The faces on Mount Rushmore.

But it was exactly for these reasons that Borglum was intrigued. Although he had created a body of work that would have satisfied most artists—including his famous head of Abraham Lincoln that stood in the Capitol Building rotunda—Borglum had yet to create his magnum opus. And at his age, it was time he gave thought to it. The Stone Mountain Memorial might have been, but Borglum was quarreling with its sponsors, and work was behind schedule.

The very remoteness of the Black Hills also appealed to Borglum. There was the challenge of finding a mountain on which he could create faces that would be colossal in size, inspirational and patriotic. Borglum believed that if he found one, the public would be so captivated by the idea that money would be forthcoming, roads would be built, and millions of people would come to see his masterwork. The Black Hills, moreover, had some of the world's oldest and hardest granite. Geologists had calculated that the stone eroded at the rate of less than half an inch every ten thousand years. An artist looking for a canvas on which to create an everlasting work could hardly have picked a better site.

Borglum met with Robinson in 1924 and studied the historian's concept of a memorial to such Western heroes as Meriwether Lewis, William Clark, Kit Carson, and "Buffalo Bill" Cody. Borglum was a patriot, but he was a realist, too. He told Robinson that money for the faces would be raised more easily if the memorial was national rather than regional in appeal. Instead of Western heroes, why not the faces of George Washington, Thomas Jefferson, and Abraham Lincoln? Robinson agreed, as did United States Senator Peter Norbeck and Congressman William Williamson of South Dakota, who got Congress to approve the memorial in the federally controlled Black Hills, although no money was appropriated. It is believed the fourth face, that of Theodore Roosevelt, was Norbeck's idea.

Borglum later explained the choices: "Jefferson appears on Mount Rushmore because he drew the Declaration of Independence; Washington because he was the great presiding officer in shaping the Constitution; Lincoln, because it was Lincoln, and no other than Lincoln, whose mind, heart, and finally life determined that we should continue as a common family of states and in union forever. Roosevelt is joined with the others because he completed the dreams of Columbus, opened the way to the East, joined the waters of the great East and West seas. Roosevelt did more; alone he stayed the encroachment of organized privilege against the principles of a government by, of, and for the people, declaring 'so far and no farther can you go with safety to the principles of a people's government.' "

Had the faces been suggested today, there is no doubt the proposal would have been buried under an avalanche of protests from conservationists. As it was, the Rapid City *Daily Journal* said the beauty of the Black Hills would be defaced, and the newspaper argued against "any alteration in nature's handiwork." Other newspaper editors agreed. Nor were gold miners and hunters especially eager to see tourists swarming into the area.

The lack of funding and the apparent lack of interest of most South Dakotans failed to discourage the bald sculptor with the shaggy mustache, who was soon confronted with new problems. Borglum's South Dakota visit irritated officials of the Stone Mountain Confederate Monumental Association, who thought he should be spending his time working on their mountain instead of running off to the Black Hills to begin carving another. In February 1925 the Association voted to fire Borglum and to bring in stonecutters to finish the job. Infuriated, Borglum destroyed his plaster models. The Association filed property-destruction charges against him, but Borglum fled Georgia before he could be arrested. The Stone Mountain group hired another sculptor, but the memorial was never completed.

Borglum began sculpting presidential faces in his San Antonio, Texas, studio before returning to South Dakota the following August to look for a suitable mountain. Ted Shoemaker, a former sheriff, was chosen as guide, and the scouting party set out into the wilderness with packhorses. Borglum took along his thirteen-year-old son, Lincoln. Although there were plenty of mountainsides from which to choose, Borglum was looking for a special one. It had to be tall enough so that the faces could be seen for miles. It must have a broad expanse of granite that was as free as possible from fissures and other inperfections. Most of all, the mountain must stand in sunlight so that the faces could be seen for most of the day. The famous Needles were not satisfactory because their spires did not offer enough working surface. Harney Peak, the highest mountain east of the Rockies, was ruled out because it was too precipitous and did not have the desired surface.

After searching for about two weeks, Borglum focused his binoculars on the shoulder of a mountain that faced southeast and caught the desired sunlight. Shoemaker said the mountain had been called Slaughterhouse Rock when Wild Bill Hickok and Calamity Jane, the frontierswoman, lived in the area. It was later named after Charles E. Rushmore, a New York City attorney who had admired its beauty while he was visiting the Black Hills.

From a distance, Mount Rushmore looked ideal. The next step was to study it up close. It took nearly two days to scale Rushmore. When they were about 150 feet from the top, they saw the rest of the way was almost straight up. Forming a pyramid by standing on each other's shoulders, the topmost man looped a lariat over a projecting sliver of granite. They pulled themselves to the top while hoping the rock would not snap off.

Borglum was exhilarated by the view from the wind-swept moun-

Mount Rushmore before the sculpturing.

taintop that stood more than a mile above sea level and was five hundred feet taller than those around it. He was even more pleased when they lowered him over the side to examine the rock. It measured about a thousand feet horizontally and four hundred feet vertically. There appeared to be plenty of good, workable stone. There was no question about it. This was *the* mountain.

But there were other questions, and very difficult ones, indeed. How would they get working gear and supplies to Rushmore? And how would they generate power for operating their equipment? The nearest settlement was the gold-mining village of Keystone, three miles away. Only a wagon trail led from there to a footpath into the thick forest. Borglum was ever one to consider problems as mere details to be overcome. He said they would simply have to gather their supplies and equipment, including a power generator, at Keystone and cut a supply road through the forest to the worksite. Then they would rig a hoist to lift their equipment to the top of Mount Rushmore. All this was an expensive proposition. Where was the money to come from? Borglum had an answer for that one, too. The important thing, he said, was to get started. Once it became public knowledge that he was proceeding, money would follow.

Borglum was right. When he dedicated the site a week later, October 1, 1925, about three thousand people were so intrigued that they came from many miles away to follow the trail to Mount Rushmore to watch the ceremony. Borglum said his four faces would be scaled to men standing 465 feet tall, or about as tall as a four-story building. He planned to make each face about sixty feet long from forehead to chin and to complete the figures down to their waists. Washington would be the most prominent in the grouping. The cost? Between $800,000 and $900,000. (Borglum's estimate was only slightly off. The faces cost $989,993.22, most of it from Federal appropriations.)

Borglum said he needed $50,000 to get started. Schoolchildren made some of the earliest contributions. The Rapid City Commercial Club raised $250, and the city's newspaper switched its position and supported the project. While money trickled in, a most fortunate coincidence occurred. President Calvin Coolidge announced his plan to make his summer White House at the state game lodge in the Black Hills.

Norbeck, the consummate politician, hit on an idea: Get Coolidge to dedicate the project. Never mind that it had already been dedicated. With the prestige of the office of the President behind the memorial, fund-raising would be easier, and Norbeck could probably engineer a money bill through Congress. Coolidge agreed to dedicate, and fund-raising spurted. It was not long before area businessmen contributed the balance of the $50,000 needed. When Coolidge arrived in South Dakota in June 1927, Borglum hired a pilot to fly him over the summer White House. The airplane swooped low, and Borglum tossed a bouquet of mountain flowers for Mrs. Coolidge onto the lawn.

Borglum meanwhile was joined by Jesse G. Tucker, his assistant on the Stone Mountain project, and they hired sixteen Keystone gold miners to help them. Tucker, a skilled carpenter, began by building a

Four workmen on Washington's nose.

shed to house a huge diesel-powered generator that had been donated anonymously. (Borglum suspected it came from the public utilities tycoon Samuel Insull.) Speed was essential if they were to make the Coolidge dedication in August before the President returned to Washington. Notations on daily work reports urged, "RUSH MORE."

Power lines from the generator were strung through the forest to a campsite in a ravine at the foot of Rushmore. Trees were felled to clear a supply road into the area. Pneumatic jackhammers, drills, and other equipment began to come in by packhorses. An old log cabin was converted into a studio for Borglum. It had a picture-window view of Rushmore. Tucker and his crew built a five-hundred-step wooden stairway that wound to the mountaintop. From the base camp, 1,400 feet of three-inch air hose for supplying the pneumatic tools was hauled to a second site of sheds built atop Rushmore.

Work was completed the day before the dedication. On August 10, 1927, Coolidge rode a horse to Rushmore. His cowboy boots and floppy hat seemed to embarrass the staid New Englander. Borglum welcomed the Chief Executive with a salute that was not only befitting a President but practical as well. Twenty-one tree stumps were blasted away to hail Coolidge as well as to push the supply road still deeper into the forest.

During the ceremony, Borglum was lowered over the side of the mountain in one of the leather-and-steel safety saddle seats he had designed for the Stone Mountain project. He made four borings with as many drills and presented one of them to the President, one to Norbeck, and another to Robinson; he kept the fourth for himself. In his speech, Coolidge said, "We have come here to dedicate a cornerstone that was laid by the hand of the Almighty."

During the next weeks, a cableway for hauling equipment from the base camp to the top of Rushmore was finished. Hand-operated winches were anchored in the mountaintop and readied for lowering and rising the workers in their safety harnesses. Lincoln Borglum, meanwhile, arrived from San Antonio with the presidential models of clay, which Borglum proceeded to convert into larger ones made of plaster of Paris. When Washington's face was five feet tall, the job of transferring the model's measurements to Mount Rushmore began.

Borglum started with a thirty-inch movable bar that he attached to the top of the head of the studio model. Fitted onto the bar was a cir-

Working on Jefferson's head.

cular plate marked with the degrees of the compass. A plumb bob was attached to the end of the bar. Similarly, a thirty-foot swinging boom with a compass plate and a plumb bob was mounted on top of Rushmore at the site of Washington's head, just as the boom would later be set into the heads of the three other faces. One inch on the model equaled twelves inches on the face. The angles of the facial features were determined by a series of intricate triangulations using the bar, compass plate, and plumb bob in the studio and converting the measurements onto the mountain. This part of the work was known as pointing, and Lincoln Borglum became expert at it.

The first step in these conversions was to locate the tip of the nose. This task seemed simple enough, but was, in fact, incredibly difficult and time-consuming. Part of the problem was that the granite often was not as good as it appeared to be. Although Borglum had hoped to avoid using dynamite, as he had learned to do on Stone Mountain, there was no other way to reach a suitable working surface. Washington's face had to be set twenty-five feet into the mountain, and parts of Jefferson and Lincoln would have to be blasted and chipped 120 feet.

In addition, there were four large fissures discovered about seventy feet apart and at forty-five-degree angles. Borglum had to position the faces to avoid them. From an esthetic viewpoint, however, Borglum constantly tilted and turned the faces of his models at various times of the day to achieve the most dramatic effects from the sunlight and shadows. When the best angle was chosen, dynamiting had to go slowly. Removal of too much surface rock could ruin the desired effect, if not the entire project. "Mistakes cannot be corrected," said Borglum. "There must be no mistakes!" He was not entirely correct, as we shall shortly see.

When the rough points of the nose and facial features were located by the swinging boom's plumb bob, they were marked with dabs of paint. Drillers bored vertical holes from two to six feet deep and inserted dynamite charges. Workers were cleared from the area at noon and four o'clock daily, when the dynamite was set off. Like thunder, the booming echoed across the Black Hills as chunks of granite went hurtling to the bottom of the ravine amid swirling clouds of dust. Gradually, an off-white, oval-shaped hump began to appear. New measurements were made, and more charges were placed.

"I often used to watch this blasting in utter amazement," said a

Gutzon Borglum frequently rode the cable car which took men and tools to the working area.

friend of Borglum, Robert J. Dean, in his book, *Living Granite*. "Every time a charge of dynamite was exploded, I saw a new portion of a face appear. It was almost like a miracle, as though an invisible creative hand, working with unseen tools, was suddenly, at one stroke, bringing life out of a dead mass. And as I watched this miracle, day after day, I began to realize the genius that was Borglum." Eventually, more than 450,000 tons of rock were blasted away. The pile still lies in a heap beneath the faces.

After blasting to within a few inches of the working surface, drillers wearing safety harnesses were lowered by steel cables over the side and began their machine-gun-like staccato chipping away at the rock with pneumatic jackhammers. When they wanted to be raised or lowered, they told a callboy who was suspended in a cage nearby. He telephoned the order to one of the winchmen on top of the mountain. Marks along the cable enabled the winchman to determine how many feet he would have to raise or lower the workman. As the faces progressed, scaffolding was hammered together and wood cages were built for workers, who peppered the faces with a honeycomb of holes bored several inches apart. Then they broke off the last remaining stone with wedging and other tools. There was no doubt of the hardness of the granite. At the peak of the work, four hundred drills were resharpened each day. The final touching-up was done with bumpers—pneumatic tools with four-point bits that smoothed the facial features. All the while, Borglum would be examining the work up close, or standing atop Iron Mountain, four miles away, as he studied Rushmore through binoculars. Here another slice needed to be chipped off, he would decide. There a gouge had to be made to achieve the desired effect.

But all of this was far in the future when work was started on Washington's face early in October, 1927, a few weeks after Coolidge's dedication. There would be many problems between the initial dynamiting on Washington and the final bumping work on Roosevelt. The most immediate need was money. By December 7, 1927, when work stopped because of subzero weather, the $50,000 had been spent. The only indication of what it had been used for was a gash on the side of the mountain.

Work would not be resumed for eighteen months. Borglum went back to working on other commissions, while Senator Norbeck intensified his efforts for a Federal appropriation. His was no easy task.

Lincoln's head is nearly done as workers, standing on scaffolding set into granite, use bumping tools to smooth and finish the stone.

Democrats blocked his money bill and said they preferred that the face of Woodrow Wilson be substituted for Theodore Roosevelt's. Suffragists wanted neither; they argued for Susan B. Anthony's. The Democrats at last relented after assurance that there would never be an admission charge to the memorial. On Washington's Birthday, 1929, Congress voted $250,000 on a matching basis, with the matching funds soon afterward being appropriated by the South Dakota legislature, which also approved funds for construction of a highway to Mount Rushmore.

The money came none too soon. Eight months later, the New York stock market collapsed, and the United States was plunged into its worst depression ever. Borglum nevertheless got right to work that summer until wintry weather halted work for the year. Washington's forehead was by then nearly completed, and his eyebrows and nose were being formed. Borglum resumed work the following spring. He concentrated on Washington's face in preparation for its dedication, while Jefferson's, to the left of it as viewed from the valley, was being blocked out.

Washington's face was dedicated on the Fourth of July, 1930. A crowd of 2,500 gathered in the valley. A huge American flag made by the women of Keystone was draped over the face. The swinging boom pulled it away to reveal Washington's sixty-foot-tall face, with eleven-foot-wide eyes and an eighteen-foot mouth. A military band struck up patriotic music while airplanes flying overhead dipped their wings. Borglum, the master public relations man, orchestrated his dedications with the intention of getting as much publicity as possible from them. Publicity could be counted on to translate into funding. The crowd cheered lustily that day, but the celebration was premature. The building fund was petering out. A year later, December 31, 1931, there was only eleven dollars left, and in those Depression times there was not much enthusiasm for faces on a mountainside, however patriotic they might be.

But there was a solution to the problem, and Norbeck found it in the Depression itself. Federal funds were available to employ the jobless, and the Mount Rushmore workers qualified. Drillers were paid only sixty-five cents an hour, and at that for only the six or seven weeks of the working season, but they were happy to get it, and Borglum could show that the memorial was proceeding, if slowly.

Borglum concentrated on Jefferson as he dynamited into the

The unveiling of Lincoln's head, September 17, 1937.

mountainside toward a suitable working surface. After blast upon blast, he began to fear that he was in trouble. And he was. With ninety feet of rock blown away, Borglum discovered a large crack which left no doubt that there was insufficient good granite to continue. The Jefferson face was abandoned, and the swinging boom was relocated at a site to the right of Washington, as seen from the valley.

It was a costly mistake, but one that Borglum could not have avoided. Jefferson's face was dynamited off the side of the mountain, and at least $10,000 in building funds and many months of work went crashing down into the ravine. Upset as he was by the loss of money and time, Borglum had no way of knowing that the mistake would pay dividends. The relocation of Jefferson's face achieved two unexpected results: Washington stood out more prominently, and the afternoon sun coming from behind Washington emphasized the shadows on Jefferson's face, thus enhancing its overall appearance.

Even at that, Jefferson gave Borglum more trouble than any of the other faces. After Jefferson was pointed and fairly well blocked out, a slanting natural crack was discovered smack where his right nostril was planned. To anybody but Borglum, the crack would have been ignored. It could not be seen from the ground, and was so small that it would not cause Jefferson nose problems until hundreds of years of erosion wore it away. Somebody apparently made the mistake of mentioning these points to Borglum, who wrote, "I have no intention of leaving a head on that mountain that in the course of five hundred or five thousand years will be without a nose." Borglum reset Jefferson's head by turning it five degrees north, tilting it eighteen inches, and moving it back four feet. The crack remains but presents no problem, as it runs alongside Jefferson's nose. Each autumn, workers are lowered over the side of the mountain and use a mixture of cement and water to reseal this and other cracks against cold weather.

Jefferson was growing steadily more recognizable when Lincoln's face was blocked out in 1935. Much to the satisfaction of Borglum and his workers, who had to climb the five-hundred-step stairway every day, an aerial cable car lift was built to haul workers and supplies. The money for it was part of that released by President Franklin D. Roosevelt in 1934, when he placed the Mount Rushmore memorial under the jurisdiction of the National Park Service of the United States Department of the Interior.

Visitors increased each year as roads were improved. There were 135,000 of them in 1933 and nearly 200,000 in 1936. From their vantage point in the valley, they stood fascinated while watching what appeared to be pygmyish workers bumping the finishing touches on Washington's eighteen-foot lower lip. And they marveled at the bluish effect Borglum had achieved in Jefferson's eyes. Borglum told visitors he had "sprinkled a little bit of sun in each eye." In effect, he had. Borglum did it by his constant assessment of progress while studying Rushmore from mountaintops miles away. It was by his genius and his painstaking attention to detail that he was able to blend sunlight and shadows to create amazing effects on Rushmore.

Borglum drove his workers hard. It might be expected that an artist constantly bothered by lack of money and an abbreviated working season would have taken shortcuts. Exactly the opposite was true, especially with regard to safety. Not one worker was killed during the project, despite the dynamiting and the high-altitude work. Borglum's safety harnesses were primarily responsible, and he also provided workers with masks to avoid the inhalation of granite dust. Consequently, there were only two noteworthy accidents.

Around two o'clock in the afternoon of Thursday, August 20, 1936, workers were drenched by a rainstorm accompanied by thunder and lightning. There had been storms before, and nobody paid much attention to them as work continued. Suddenly, a lightning bolt detonated some dynamite caps. Three workers were stunned, one of whom had his shoes blown off. The other accident occurred while the cable car was coming down the aerial tramway with workers and equipment. Losing its brakes, the car gathered speed as it zipped down the quarter-mile steel cable. Happy Anderson leaped out. Another worker jammed a steel bar under a pulley and braked the car as it slammed into the base terminal. Only Anderson suffered serious injuries.

Jefferson was dedicated on August 30, 1936, ten days after the lightning accident. President Roosevelt arrived that afternoon, to be greeted by a cheering crowd of thousands. A sixty-foot flag hung over Jefferson while the National Anthem was played. Borglum set off a ceremonial dynamite blast, and the flap was stripped away by the swinging boom. A small plane dropped tiny parachutes with souvenir stone chips from Rushmore. Roosevelt was not scheduled to speak, but he was so moved by what he saw above him on Rushmore that he changed his mind. "This can be a monument and an inspiration for the continuance of the democratic republican form of government, not only for our own beloved country, but, we hope, throughout the world," said the President.

Borglum turned sixty-nine years old in 1936, and with that came the realization that he had been working on Rushmore for nine years, far longer than he had expected. His fervent dedication was profound—indeed, some of his associates thought him a man obsessed. But was there enough time left to him to finish the memorial? Borglum sadly realized his own mortality even more when Norbeck died that year; he thus lost his champion in Congress. But Borglum put aside such thoughts, beefed up his working crew, and set fifty men to working on Lincoln.

The face of Lincoln is the best example of Borglum's uncanny ability to combine sunlight and shadows against rock. Borglum directed the drillers as they recessed the pupils of Lincoln's eyes so that they remained in the shadows. While chipping away in the eye sockets, they created twenty-two-inch-long slivers of rock that reflect sunlight. The result makes Lincoln seem to be alive, as was obvious to everybody attending the dedication of the face, September 17, 1937, on the 150th anniversary of the ratification of the United States Constitution.

Theodore Roosevelt's face, meanwhile, was blocked out, but came very close to going the way of the first Jefferson. The granite was found to be unworkable until Borglum's workers penetrated 120 feet into the rock. The old bugaboo—lack of money—was a problem again by 1938. The suffragists spoke out once again for Susan B. Anthony, but this time Borglum had an answer: there was no more space remaining on Rushmore, and in fact he was being forced to cut Roosevelt's face pretty thin.

Congress voted an additional $300,000 in 1938, and Borglum concentrated on Roosevelt's face while starting a Hall of Records which, he said, would house "all important records of our civilization." The hall also was to contain twenty-five large statues, including Susan B. Anthony's. Borglum started to blast an opening into the canyon behind the faces, but got only as far as a short entryway before abandoning the tunnel to mountain goats, which sometimes use it for winter shelter.

Borglum seemed to sense that time was running out on him while as many as thirty workers labored on the mountain that year. For the first time, he kept his crews working through the winter, while being shielded from snowstorms and icy winds by canvas shrouds over their scaffolding. Air-compressor lines froze, and workers had to take frequent breaks to warm themselves around stoves in the mountaintop sheds. It was a miserable time for everybody, but all of that was forgotten the following July 2, 1939, when Roosevelt was dedicated on the fiftieth anniversary of South Dakota's statehood.

This fourth and final dedication, made at night under a full moon and a clear sky, was more spectacular than the earlier ones. Some twelve thousand people attended. Sioux Indians sang and danced, and silent-movie star William S. Hart performed. Then came a blazing display of fireworks and aerial bombs. When the last rockets flamed out, the four faces on Mount Rushmore were suddenly lit by powerful searchlights in the valley. Borglum's pride that night was matched only by that of eighty-four-year-old Doane Robinson. (Permanent floodlights were installed in 1950; they light the faces from

George Washington.

Theodore Roosevelt.

Thomas Jefferson.

Abraham Lincoln.

June 1 to Labor Day for night visitors among the two million people who visit Mount Rushmore annually.)

Much work remained to be done. Two years later, October 31, 1941, Lincoln Borglum set off the final dynamite blast. Washington had been completed down to his collar and lapels. Jefferson's collar was blocked out. Finishing touches had refined Lincoln's head, but parts of Roosevelt's face remained incomplete. And that is the way the four faces on Mount Rushmore would remain.

On March 6, 1941, seven months before that final blast on Rushmore, Gutzon Borglum died of a heart attack in a Chicago hospital. Borglum's frequent reply to those who marveled at the faces on Mount Rushmore became as enduring as the memorial itself. "The faces were always there," he said. "I just uncovered them."

VIII

Hoover Dam

THE COLORADO RIVER was one of the most dangerous in the world. Snow melting in the Rocky Mountains in spring and early summer regularly sent floodwaters rampaging with the speed of an express train down the Colorado and into the low-lying valleys of Southern California and Arizona. The worst flood occurred in 1884, when 384,000 cubic feet of water per second stormed down the river. Almost as bad were the 1905-1907 flash floods which spilled into Southern California's Imperial Valley to create the Salton Sea. Thousands of acres of some of the richest agricultural land in the world were inundated, farms were destroyed, highways were ruined, and the Southern Pacific Railroad tracks linking California with the East were washed away.

Flooding was but one of the river's treacheries. With the possible exception of the Tigris River in southwest Asia, the Colorado was more heavily laden with sediment than any other. This silt turned the water a reddish brown color and give the Colorado its nickname, the Red Bull. In an average year, hundreds of thousands of tons of silt came down the river—enough to cover 214 square miles of land to a depth of one foot. This silt clogged irrigation canals and ditches and spread an impervious coating over the farmlands. Removal costs were in the millions. The Colorado also was capricious. The river was the sole source of water for people living around it. When the flood season ended, the river's flow often fell off to a mere trickle. Livestock perished, entire crops withered and died in the desert heat.

Aerial view looking north to Hoover Dam and Lake Mead.

This water feast-or-famine cycle had gone on for centuries along the river, which began high in the Rockies of north central Colorado and followed a zigzagging course in a southwesterly direction for more than 1,400 miles before emptying into the Gulf of California. During its race to the gulf, the powerful Colorado had gouged deep canyons through the arid wastelands, including the 217-mile-long Grand Canyon. The cycle might have continued, except for the rapid growth of population in the Southwest starting shortly after 1900, when many farming communities were established in California's Imperial and Coachella valleys.

The future of the region depended upon finding solutions to the flooding and sedimentation problems, as well as on providing for a guaranteed year-round supply of water, plus low-cost power. If these problems could be solved, then the valleys would provide the United States with a major supply of fruits and vegetables. Industries would be attracted, and the entire Southwest would prosper.

Attempts to harness the river started around the time of the Civil War. The only answer was a dam. It would have to be taller than any in the world, and it would present architectural, engineering and construction challenges unparalleled in the history of mankind. Actual search for a site started in 1901 and gathered momentum the following year with the creation of what is now the Bureau of Reclamation in the United States Department of the Interior.

The site criteria included a large area upstream from the dam where the flow from the Colorado and its upper tributaries could be trapped and stored until needed for downstream irrigation and for domestic use as well as for power generation. Reclamation engineers calculated that requirements called for a deep reservoir that could hold two years' average flow of the Colorado. The reservoir would solve the sedimentation problem because it would serve as a massive settling basin.

To control the flow of the water past the dam—and to prevent water from overrunning it—would require a system of intake towers, tunnels and spillways. Somewhere downstream, a canal would have to be built to carry water to the Imperial and Coachella valleys. A dam of this magnitude offered an opportunity to build a hydroelectric generating plant that would stand as one of the world's largest. This powerplant added still another requirement for the dam: it would have to be located where it would be economically feasible to transmit power to major markets, especially energy-hungry Los Angeles.

Reclamation Bureau engineers and United States Geological Survey teams studied seventy possible sites in that remote desert that is sometimes called the American Sahara. It was a time-consuming, dangerous and difficult job, as the teams were lowered into rugged canyons to make test drillings and topographical maps. Three men were killed during this work. Site-location efforts were spurred in 1916, when a devastating flood from the combined waters of the Colorado and Gila rivers swept into Arizona's Yuma valley.

Aerial view looking across Hoover Dam from the Arizona side. Highway 93, one of the most heavily traveled highways in the western United States, crosses Hoover Dam.

In 1919 teams began to study Black Canyon (also known as Lower Boulder Canyon). Black Canyon forms a boundry between Arizona and Nevada and is about thirty miles southeast of Las Vegas. The V-shaped canyon was more than 700 feet deep, around 300 feet wide at the bottom, and more than 900 feet across at the top. Test drillings found that volcanic rock was suitably hard. Bedrock for the dam could be reached by going down only between 110 and 150 feet. Black Canyon had similarly excellent rock for many miles up and down the river. This feature would provide sturdy abutments for the dam and the deep reservoir.

Selection of Black Canyon was relatively easy compared to the legislative and legal hurdles. The mighty basin of the Colorado includes parts or all of seven states: Arizona, California, Colorado, Nevada, New Mexico, Utah, and Wyoming, a total land mass representing about thirteen percent of the United States. While all seven states realized the need to tame the Red Bull, any proposal for tampering with their vital water supply demanded serious consideration and a guarantee that each state would have enough for its present and future needs. Of major concern to Arizona and other states was the fear that California, with its hundreds of thousands of irrigable acres, would severely drain the Colorado, thus depriving Arizona's Yuma Valley and other areas of the region.

Construction of the dam threatened to be stymied for years by litigation over water rights. In 1920 a commission was formed from representatives of the seven states, with Secretary of Commerce Herbert Hoover serving as chairman. Hoover suggested a compromise: Divide the Colorado River region into Upper and Lower basins. The water would be equitably apportioned in perpetuity between the two basins with no single state receiving an exactly prescribed amount. The actual amount of water to be apportioned could be decided later by future agreements among the states.

The Hoover Compromise was approved by the commission, and from it came the Colorado River Compact, which was signed by the members on November 24, 1922, in Santa Fe, New Mexico. The matter then went to the legislatures of the seven states for ratification. Six quickly ratified, but Arizona held out until February 1944. This dispute over the division of water finally was resolved by the United States Supreme Court in 1962, more than a quarter of a century after the dam was finished. The Colorado River Compact is one of the

An overhead crane in the powerplant at Hoover Dam lowers the giant rotor into the stator of the generating unit which produced Hoover Dam's first commercial hydroelectric energy October 26, 1936.

landmark pieces of legislation in the history of the United States and is a model for similar regional agreements.

The compact cleared the way for building the dam. On December 21, 1928, Congress passed the Boulder Canyon Project Act, authorizing the construction of the dam and the canal linking the Colorado with the Imperial and Coachella valleys. The act declared that the Colorado Compact became effective with ratification by six of the seven states. A provision held that California must agree to exercise discretion in tapping the Colorado to prevent other basin states from suffering. The act also appropriated $165 million for construction.

Except for $25 million that was allocated for flood control, the money was to be repaid with three percent interest in fifty years from revenues derived from the sale of electric power. Repayment of the flood-control money was deferred for later congressional action.

Contracts for supplying power generated at Hoover Dan were quickly negotiated by 1930. Under the original agreements, the Metropolitan Water District of Southern California, serving more than one hundred communities, was entitled to buy thirty-five percent of the energy; the City of Los Angeles Department of Water and Power, seventeen percent; the states of Arizona and Nevada, seventeen percent; Southern California Edison Company, nearly eight percent; and the remainder to Glendale and Pasadena, California. These contracts significantly encouraged the start of the dam.

Congress in that year named the project Hoover Dam, in recognition of Herbert Hoover's significant role. Hoover was then President. (It is a curious offshoot of the story of Hoover Dam that the Republican President became a scapegoat for the Great Depression that beset the nation in 1929. In May 1933, before the first concrete was poured at the dam, Interior Secretary Harold L. Ickes, under the Democratic administration of President Franklin D. Roosevelt, changed the name to Boulder Dam, and it is by this name that many people know it today. In April 1947, however, the 80th Congress restored the original name, and Hoover Dam it is.)

There were many who opposed the project. Not a little of the debate focused on the Federal government's right to interfere in matters which some said belonged to the states. This was the era before the Tennessee Valley Authority and other federally directed regional projects became commonplace. The states' righters wanted no part of Washington interference in their affairs, however necessary it might be, and however ineffective the resources of individual states were in finding solutions to their common problems.

A number of experts said the project was doomed to failure. In the first place, construction of the dam required that the Colorado be completely diverted around the worksite. Changing the course of the mighty Colorado was something man had been trying to do since 1540, when the river was discovered by the Spanish explorer Hernando de Alarcón. After centuries of attempts, nobody had succeeded. A committee of engineers presented one of the more critical reports: "It is obvious that the proposed program and the estimated costs are all but impossible. The material must all be handled in a narrow canyon, with high, precipitous walls, with a raging river at the bottom. It is at least questionable whether enough men and equipment could be put into the restricted space to accomplish the task within the required time, even if the work was done without any regard for cost."

Even the Reclamation engineers admitted there were imponderables which raised legitimate questions. Would the energy market, especially in Southern California, grow sufficiently large to absorb all the power that could be generated and thus make the project economically feasible? Building the dam would be a race against the unpredictable river, especially at the beginning. If diversion tunnels and cofferdams holding back the water from invading the working surface of the dam were not finished before early spring and summer floods, the coffers could be washed away, especially if luck turned against them and the floods ran far beyond seasonal norms. Luck would play a strong factor, and that was an intangible no engineer's slide rule could possibly measure.

In addition, Black Canyon lay in an earthquake zone. Although tests showed no recent seismological activity, some engineers raised the question of whether the massive weight of the fluctuating water in the reservoir could set off a chain reaction by shaking the earth's crust, thus causing an earthquake. If an earthquake occurred, or if for some reason this concrete dam of a size never before attempted by man collapsed, a 500-foot wall of water would go cascading down the gorge and cause a disaster the likes of which the United States had never known. At least five cities would be destroyed, including Yuma. The battering ram of water would cause irreparable damage in the Imperial Valley and gouge a permanent channel to the Salton Sea.

The magnitude of the project was too much for the Reclamation Bureau alone. If Hoover Dam was to be built, it would have to be done through the combined efforts of the Federal government and private industry. But what company would undertake such a formidable challenge, especially considering the potential for disaster inherent in the project? If the dam came crashing down, the resulting lawsuits would mean certain financial ruin for a company.

Interior Secretary Ray Lyman Wilbur said to the pessimists: "In controlled water lies the future of our country, and particularly that of its western portion. The Hoover Dam will signalize our national conquest over the Great American Desert. With dollars, men and engineering plans, we will build a great natural resource; we will make new geography and start a new era in the southwestern part of the United States. With Imperial Valley no longer menaced by floods, new hopes and new financial credit will be given to one of the largest irrigation districts in the West. By increasing the water supply of Los Angeles and surrounding cities, homes and industries are made possible for many millions of people. A great new source of power forecasts the coming of new lines and the creation of new industries in Arizona, Nevada and California. I view this great Colorado River project as a portent of new thinking and of new methods for the future advancement of our country." Supremely confident that the extensive testing proved that Hoover Dam could be built, Secretary Wilbur on July 7, 1930, told Dr. Elwood Mead, head of the Reclamation Bureau, to start construction.

There was much preliminary work before the dam could be started. From a working viewpoint, a worse site could not have been picked. Black Canyon was surrounded by miles of desert inhabited by gila monsters and rattlesnakes. Temperatures hit 125 degrees, and thermal drafts coming out of Black Canyon were even hotter. There were no railroads or highways into the area, no power to operate equipment or supply lighting for the work which would proceed around the clock. Workers would have to be recruited throughout the United States, and a complete desert city built to house them and care for their needs.

Construction materials would come mostly by rail. On September 17, 1930, a branch line was started from what is now the Union Pacific Railroad at Bracken, south of Las Vegas. More than thirty miles of track were laid by the Union Pacific and the Reclamation Bureau to the dam site by February 5, 1931. It was estimated that twenty locomotives would be kept busy hauling in some 63,000 carloads of materials on this line, which was named the United States Construction Railroad. The Reclamation Bureau reported: "Materials would be required in quantities never before shipped to a single construction job in so short a time—five million barrels of cement, eighteen million pounds of structural steel, twenty-one million pounds of (water) gates and valves, and 840 miles of pipe." Construction of roads began around Black Canyon while a power transmission line was being strung more than 200 miles across the mountains and

View of Hoover Dam from the Nevada Powerhouse ramp.

desert from a San Bernardino, California, substation. The power line was completed on June 25, 1931.

Early that year, the Reclamation Bureau started work on the city to house workers and their families. Heat around Black Canyon was too intense to build Boulder City at the worksite. A high plateau seven miles to the southwest was selected because of its more moderate climate. Workers would commute to the dam by a highway that also had to be built. Boulder City was laid out in the shape of a triangle. Water was pumped from the Colorado, power lines strung, and, as if by magic, a model city with paved streets and parkways, trees, flowers, schools, churches, a playground, and a swimming pool rose as an oasis in the middle of the desert.

Boulder City would have all the amenities of a small town: family homes and bachelor quarters, a movie theater, stores, dentists, doctors, a mortician, a police force, a fire department, and a cafeteria that could feed 1,300 workers at a time. The government carefully screened requests from merchants and others throughout the United States who applied to open businesses in Boulder City. Unlike the early frontier towns of the West and their infamous lawlessness, Boulder City would not tolerate undesirables. Laws were rigidly enforced, and punishment was the worst possible for a man who needed work: loss of his job and eviction from Boulder City.

With national unemployment rising sharply during the Depression, President Hoover had in 1930 directed Reclamation engineers in their main design office in Denver to expedite specifications so the job could be put out to bid earlier than planned. Hoover Dam would have an economic impact on every state, because each would supply something to the project. It was calculated that for every ten workers employed at the dam, eighteen more would find work in the factories of suppliers. Economists say Hoover Dam had a negligible effect on lowering unemployment, but the fact that an estimated 46,000 families would be fed, clothed and housed from expenditures on Hoover Dam had at least a salutary effect upon the nation's sagging morale.

When the Bureau of Reclamation put the job out for bid, it explained that the Federal government would purchase most of the building materials and assume financial responsibility for all flood risks until the cofferdams were built. Six bids were received and opened on March 4, 1931. The lowest bid, $48,890,995.50, was submitted by Six Companies, Inc., of San Francisco, a group of major contracting firms: the Utah Construction Company; the Pacific Bridge Company; Henry J. Kaiser and W. A. Bechtel Company; MacDonald & Kahn Company, Limited; Morrison-Knudsen Company; and the J. F. Shea Company. "The Big Six" offered impressive credentials: more than 4,000 successfully completed contracts, including more than 25 dams, 5,000 miles of railroad, 2,000 miles of highway, 1,800 bridges, and 275 tunnels. A week later their bid was accepted and the contract awarded. It was the largest ever made up to that time by the United States Government. Big Six was given seven years to complete the job. The company wasted no time, and, with Patrick J. Crowe named construction superintendent, Big Six was quickly on the job site. The race to tame the Red Bull was on.

Big Six opened an employment office in San Francisco. The Depression and national publicity combined to provide a large pool of qualified workers. By May, about a thousand had been hired at a minimum wage of four dollars for an eight-hour day. They camped near Black Canyon while Boulder City was being finished.

A formidable armada of the most modern construction equipment in the world was rushed to the site by Six Companies. It included 233 trucks of up to fifty-ton hauling capacity, a dozen mammoth electric shovels, draglines and other excavating machines, cranes and derricks, 115 gondola cars which could hold fifty tons of gravel apiece, and eight locomotives and people-mover trucks that could carry as many as 150 workers at a time.

Black Canyon was spanned by small work bridges. Cableways were installed along the canyon rims for lowering up to 150 tons of supplies at a time into the canyon. Machine shops were built; huge air-compressor plants for supplying pneumatic jackhammers and other equipment went up. Warehouses for supplies were built. Workers wearing safety harnesses were lowered over the canyon rims. These high-scalers began chipping away loose rock with power tools or drilled holes for dynamite charges to remove rock which could injure or kill workers when actual construction began at the bottom of the canyon. By the time they were finished, nearly one million cubic yards of rock were pried or blasted off the canyon walls.

Anticipating the demand for tremendous quantities of concrete that soon would began to be poured around the clock, Six Companies built two huge concrete-mixing facilities. A plant for screening and washing sand and gravel—the largest of its kind anywhere—

The flow of the Colorado River is being regulated through the 50-foot-diameter diversion tunnels on the Nevada side of the project.

also was constructed. When done, the plant stood ready to prepare more than sixteen tons of sand and gravel a minute for mixing with cement and water. The project's insatiable hunger for gravel would be met from pits eight miles up the river on the Arizona side of Black Canyon. Big Six built twenty miles of railroad line to the pits as well as a belt conveyer on a suspension bridge that crossed the canyon into Nevada. The conveyer belt would pour gravel into trains of gondola cars which would then be rushed to the Nevada side of the construction site.

In the incredibly short period of three months, the Big Six was far enough ahead of schedule to begin blasting the four water-diversion tunnels through Black Canyon, two on each side of the river. Each tunnel would be fifty-six feet in diameter, before being lined with three feet of concrete. The tunnels would extend about four thousand feet south through the canyon walls until they opened onto the Colorado well below the dam and powerplant site.

The tunneling job was attacked by workers standing on three-tiered mobile platforms on which were mounted batteries of compressed-air drills. Thirty-six drills simultaneously chewed into the rock to a depth of as much as twenty feet at a time. The rig was then backed out, dynamite charges were stuffed in the holes, and Black

Canyon trembled with the vibrations from the exploding dynamite. Broken rock was quickly power-scooped into huge trucks which rumbled up the construction roads from the canyon and sped to nearby canyons where the rubble was dumped. The trucks then raced back for more.

Each blast tore out about 17 feet of rock, and on one day the workers pushed the tunneling 256 feet ahead. By the time the tunnels were finished, more than three and a half million pounds of dynamite would be used to bore these tunnels, which were the second largest in the world. Each tunnel could carry more than 200,000 cubic feet of water per second.

Tunnel burrowing continued night and day as work on the upper and lower earth-and-rock-fill cofferdams was rushed to completion. The upper cofferdam would help to divert the Colorado into the tunnels and prevent water from entering the construction area of the dam. The lower cofferdam would block water from back-flowing into the worksite. This period was especially critical. Failure of the upper cofferdam due to a sudden flood would put the project in deep trouble; instead of having to excavate only silt down to bedrock to build the dam, the workers would lose many months until low-water season came, when they would have to start afresh with a new cofferdam—a job compounded by cost and the difficulty of having to remove the chunks of the demolished dam.

In February 1932 blasting and excavation started on the spillways, one on each side of the river and extending from the reservoir site to below that of the powerplant. When completed, the spillways would provide a safety valve for carrying excess water around the dam, especially during the flood season. Each spillway was sunk on a sharp incline blasted into Black Canyon until it connected with the outer diversion tunnel.

The two Arizona diversion tunnels were completed in mid-November 1932. With the help of the upper cofferdam, the course of the Colorado was successfully changed by man for the first time in history. The builders' gamble had paid off; luck was with them, and work was one year ahead of schedule. When the 1933 floods came storming down the Colorado, the cofferdams held. Water gushed through the tunnels and emptied harmlessly into the river downstream. But there was no time to celebrate, as dynamiting continued to reverberate along the deep canyon; the ground trembled with the blasts amid the constant rumbling of the heavy trucks and other construction equipment, plus the incessant chomp, chomp, chomp of the gravel-preparation plant going full bore around the clock. By July 1933 all four tunnels were done—eighteen months ahead of schedule.

With the successful diversion of the Colorado, excavation work

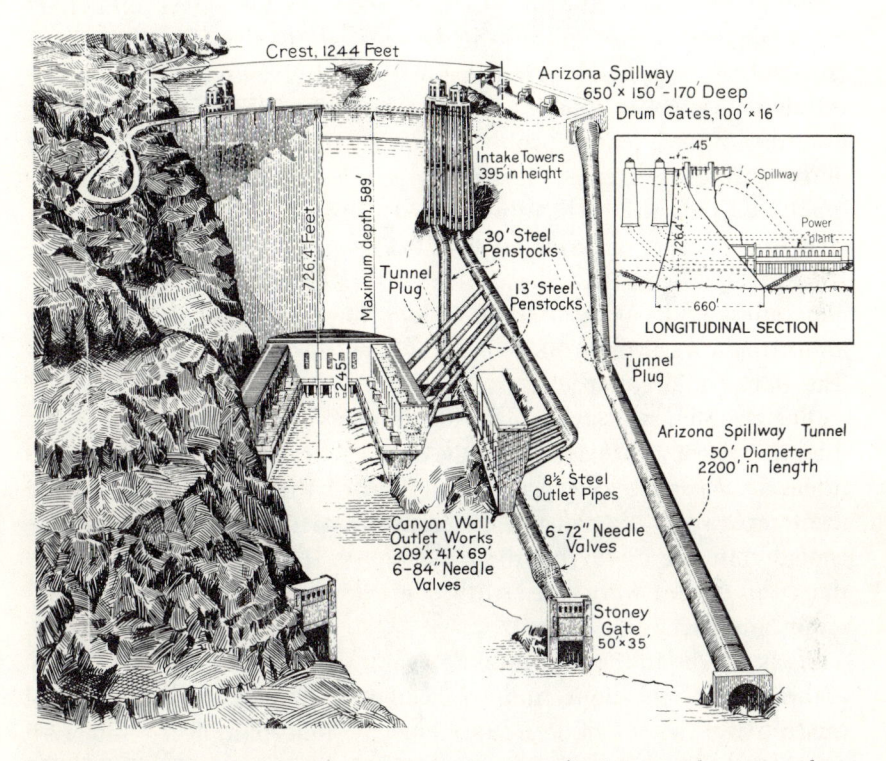

The operation of Hoover Dam is shown in this diagram. The Arizona-side cutaway shows the intake towers, spillway, penstock pipes, and outlet works. The Nevada side contains an identical system.

began at once on the dam foundations. Massive pumps drained water from the area between the cofferdams. Huge power shovels and draglines chugged in and began scooping out sediment which had lain undisturbed for centuries until bedrock was reached. After more than 500,000 cubic yards of sediment and dirt were excavated, cement-pouring preparations started.

The dam would consist of 230 interconnected building blocks between twenty-five and sixty feet square and no more than thirty feet tall. Framed with wood which would later be removed, the first pouring was made on June 6, 1933. Bucket upon bucket of concrete, each containing eight cubic yards, was dumped. By the end of the year, one million yards of concrete would be in place; by the end of the next year, two million more; and another quarter million would be poured before the final bucket on May 29, 1935.

The huge building blocks required up to thirty-six carloads of cement a day. When the job was done, the more than five million barrels of cement that went into the dam was about as much as the Reclamation Bureau had poured in the entire twenty-seven years of its construction work. Volumes of concrete poured this fast created still another unprecedented problem. The chemical reaction that occurs while concrete sets causes heating which, as concrete cools, results in cracking. This would have presented no problem in ordinary construction because concrete cools as fast as it is routinely poured. But Hoover Dam was not ordinary. Engineers estimated that the dam's concrete would not cool for up to two hundred years, thus creating an extreme hazard to the structural integrity of the concrete mass. The dam could collapse.

The problem was solved, during pouring, by inserting one-inch-diameter steel tubes horizontally and vertically at about five-foot intervals. Near-freezing water was pumped through the tubes until the temperature of the fresh concrete dropped to match that of the cooled concrete in surrounding blocks. As the concrete contracted, the open spaces were filled with cement to make the dam a solid, monolithic structure.

Work on the four water-intake towers, two on each side of the reservoir side of the dam, and connected to it by bridges, was proceeding well ahead of schedule. The 395-foot-high steel-reinforced concrete towers each had two gates for admitting water. Gigantic steel trash racks prevented debris from entering and fouling powerplant equipment. The towers would pass the water through penstocks—some of them steel pipes as large as thirty feet in diameter—to the powerplant and to discharge works downstream on both sides of the river.

Fabricating the huge penstocks raised still more problems. The Babcock & Wilcox Company of New York and Barberton, Ohio, had been awarded a $10,908,000 contract on June 15, 1932, to supply the pipes. A large share of the company's work required fabrication of two and three-quarters miles of penstocks from steel plate with a thickness of nearly three inches. These thirty-foot-diameter pipes were too heavy to be transported from the Barberton plant on conventional railroad cars. Even if they could have been, the bulky penstocks were too big to pass through tunnels.

Babcock & Wilcox solved the problem by building a gigantic fabricating plant along the United States Construction Railroad at Bechtel, Nevada, about a mile north of the dam. Flat steel plates were shipped from Barberton to Bechtel, where the penstocks were formed, welded, and X-rayed to double-check the quality of the welding. Specially constructed 200-ton trailers pulled by crawler tractors took the penstocks to the canyon rim, where they were lowered into place. The pipes were attached by steel pins, some of them as large as three inches in diameter.

Starting in June 1933, construction was pushed on transmission towers and lines to carry the power to market. The City of Los Angeles' Department of Water and Power built the two largest. They each transmitted 287,000 volts, the highest carried by any transmission line in the world at that time. The 270-mile lines to Los Angeles were strung along towers that stood as tall as 109 feet. When completed in 1936, they were at that time the largest of their kind in the world.

Meanwhile, concrete-pouring continued night and day on the steadily rising dam while work proceeded on the intake towers, penstocks and spillways. Excavations for the powerplant foundations along the downstream toe of the dam were done by January 1934. More workers were hired until, by the summer of 1934, a peak force of 5,218 men was on the job. The U-shaped powerplant began to take form, with 650-foot wings butting against each side of Black Canyon. The plant extended for 350 feet across the dam. The walls of the plant gradually rose to their full height—nearly twenty stories—and were roofed with 4½-foot-thick steel-reinforced concrete to protect against falling rocks.

Water would be fed to the turbines by a system of penstocks equipped with control gates. The seventeen turbines—about equally divided between the Arizona and Nevada wings—would have a total generating capability of 1,344,000 kilowatts. (A kilowatt is 1,000 watts, or 1.34 horsepower.) Until 1949, when Grand Coulee Dam was completed in Washington, Hoover Dam's plant stood as the most powerful anywhere, and it still ranks as one of the world's largest hydroelectric installations.

In August 1934 work began on the irrigation canal to California. Because the canal would lie entirely within the United States, it was given the name All-American Canal. The flow into the canal was controlled by a dam on the Colorado at Imperial, some 300 miles downstream from Hoover Dam and about 18 miles north of Yuma. The All-American Canal was completed in 1940 and extends 80 miles west into California near Calexico, where three branches supply the Imperial Valley. Eight years later, the Colorado's irrigation capabilities were extended 123 miles into the Coachella Valley. It takes water ten days to travel from the reservoir at Hoover Dam to the furthermost reach of the canal.

When the concrete-lined spillways were completed at Hoover Dam early in 1935, upstream plugs were placed in the outer diversion tunnels to seal them off. The fifty-foot-diameter spillways could now take over the job of providing more than adequate flood insurance. They have the capability of carrying 518,000 cubic feet of water a second at a speed of 120 miles an hour around the dam—far in excess of any known Colorado floods. Additional flood-proofing was provided when the inner diversion tunnels were similarly plugged, and two of the intake towers took over the ability to rout excess water through outlet works on each side of the canyon and through the original inner diversion tunnel outlets downstream.

With this first-time capability to control the flow of the Colorado, the Red Bull was finally tamed on February 1, 1935, when water began to rise in the reservoir. By the end of June, water stood 271 feet deep and was rising steadily. With the deep reservoir providing an ideal sediment trap, "the formerly muddy Colorado was transformed into a lake of clear blue water sparkling in the brilliant sun," reported the Bureau of Reclamation.

By that summer, the job was all but done. Six Companies had completed Hoover Dam more than two years ahead of schedule. At dedication ceremonies, September 30, 1935, President Roosevelt said, "This is an engineering victory of the first order—another great achievement of American resourcefulness, skill and determination. This is why I congratulate you who have created Boulder Dam [sic] and on behalf of the nation say to you, 'Well done!' "

A year later, September 11, 1936, President Roosevelt pushed a gold key in Washington during the World Power Conference and started up a small generator at the dam. Actual production of power

President Franklin Roosevelt is driven through a steel tunnel liner.

did not start until the following October 7, when the first 115,000 horsepower turbine began working. Two days later, power was being transmitted to Los Angeles. Additional turbines were gradually installed until the last went on-line, December 1, 1961, a quarter of a century after Hoover Dam was finished.

Hoover Dam is indeed a monument to the teamwork of the Federal government and private industry. It contains three and one-quarter million cubic yards of concrete. If that concrete was formed into a city block, it would stand taller than the Empire State Building, or pave a 16-foot-wide highway between San Francisco and New York. The dam stands 171 feet taller than the Washington National Monument. Some 92,335 tons of steel went into the dam, which weighs 6,600,000 tons.

The reservoir, named Lake Mead on February 6, 1936, after the head of the Bureau of Reclamation, extends 110 miles upstream into the Grand Canyon. Lake Mead has a 550-mile shoreline and is 500 feet at its deepest. It is the largest man-made body of water in the United States. Lake Mead holds enough water to cover the entire state of Pennsylvania to a depth of one foot, or about five thousand gallons for every person on the face of the earth.

The significance of the Hoover Dam project to the growth of the Southwest cannot be overstated. The Imperial and Coachella valleys today have an irrigable area of 608,000 acres. The Yuma Valley has around 68,000, with more than 115,000 irrigable acreage nearby. Through a treaty with Mexico, Hoover Dam supplies water to about 400,000 rich agricultural acres in that country. With a dependable water supply, the growing season is 365 days a year. These lands provide the United States and world markets with a year-round supply of fruits and vegetables of all kinds, as well as cotton, grains, and seeds. The annual value of crops in the Imperial Valley alone is around $70 million.

Thanks to the low-cost power supplied by Hoover Dam, hundreds of industries have risen from the once-barren desert, along with cities and towns. Vast reserves of minerals, including copper and titanium, are being tapped by mines operating with Hoover Dam's output. The power from Hoover Dam saves the United States about ten million barrels of oil a year that would otherwise be required to supply the needs of the area. So, too, has Southern California prospered. In addition to Los Angeles and San Diego, the Metropolitan Water District serves industrial and domestic requirements of ten million people in a four-thousand-square-mile area of Southern California.

Not the least of the beneficial fallouts of Hoover Dam was one that was only partially foreseen at the outset. Lake Mead has become one of the most popular recreational areas in the United States. At least seven million people visit the area every year to enjoy swimming, fishing, camping, boating, water-skiing and other recreational pursuits in the clear waters of Lake Mead, which is supervised by the National Park Service of the Interior Department. Lake Mead, moreover, has become a wildlife sanctuary.

In 1955 the American Society of Civil Engineers named Hoover Dam one of the seven modern civil engineering wonders of the United States. It is easy to understand why.

IX

The Golden Gate Bridge

AMONG THE FIRST to propose building a bridge across the Golden Gate was a madman who had taken the title Norton I, Emperor of the United States and Protector of Mexico. Joshua A. Norton had been a prosperous San Francisco rice speculator until business reverses drove him insane. Emperor Norton became a famous local character as he roamed the city in his regal costume, issued his own money, ate free in the best restaurants, and was mildly tolerated by the citizens, whom he considered his subjects. They were frequently amused by his outrageous proclamations. In an 1869 edict, Emperor Norton commanded his subjects to build a bridge across the mile-wide body of water which separated San Francisco from the counties to the north.

The city paid as much attention to that proclamation as they did to his others, which is to say none at all. Almost everyone was certain that it was beyond the capability of man to bridge the wide strait that explorer John Frémont had named the Golden Gate. The strait connects the Pacific Ocean with San Francisco Bay and is one of the most hazardous bodies of navigable water in the world. Golden Gate tides reverse themselves four times a day to create a massive flow seven times greater in force than the entire volume of water pouring from the mouth of the Mississippi River. Golden Gate riptides collide with San Francisco Bay ebbtides and strong Pacific Ocean currents to create swirling surges that are so violent that ships are often swept off course and are sometimes turned halfway around. If the powerful

The Golden Gate Bridge from the San Francisco side.

tides surging back and forth did not bowl the bridge over, and if some ship groping through the Golden Gate's frequent fogs did not knock it over, then certainly an earthquake would topple it, because the deadly San Andreas Fault was only a few miles away.

But there were those who thought it could be done, including Leland Stanford and Charles Crocker, two of the builders of the Southern Pacific Railroad's portion of the transcontinental railroad. The bridge would enable the railroad to directly enter San Francisco, instead of having to ferry passengers and freight across the bay. They said that if they could bridge the mighty Sierra Nevada Mountains with a railroad, then they could easily bridge the Golden Gate. But nothing came of their proposals, and the idea lay dormant until 1916, when James H. Wilkins, who had studied for a civil engineering career but found newspaper reporting more fascinating, suggested a bridge in the August 26 issue of the San Francisco *Bulletin*.

Wilkins said a tall suspension bridge would not interfere with navigation. The center span could be made "longer than any other structure of its kind in the world." He suggested that the bridge be built where the Golden Gate was the narrowest: between Fort Point in San Francisco and Lime Point on the Marin County side. And that is exactly where it would be built. Wilkins's article sparked interest, but World War I broke out a few months later, and the idea died again until the day after the war ended.

On November 12, 1918, the matter was revived before the San Francisco Board of Supervisors, who expected a price tag of about $100 million. A site study was begun, and about a dozen engineers were invited to submit designs. Among them was Joseph Baermann Strauss. Nobody knew more about building bridges than he did, although those who met the shy fifty-one-year-old civil engineer, who stood a few inches over five feet, found that hard to believe. Strauss had designed more than four hundred bridges, including the Arlington Memorial Bridge over the Potomac River, which connected the Lincoln Memorial Monument in Washington, D.C., and the Arlington National Cemetery in Virginia.

In February 1920 the United States Coast and Geodetic Survey ship *Natoma* made soundings in the Golden Gate. The report was ominous. Centuries of swirling waters had cut a gorge that was as much as 318 feet deep. "Federal experts believe it will be impossible to put piers [for the support towers of the bridge] at this point owing to strong current and great depth," reported the San Francisco *Chronicle*.

This was exactly the kind of challenge that fascinated Strauss, who proceeded to design a bridge which led many San Franciscans to wonder whether they had another Emperor Norton in their midst. Strauss designed a combination cantilever and suspension bridge. The cantilever parts of the bridge went from each shore to a point in the river where they ended in towers. The suspension part of the bridge was the part between the two towers. The bridge would be supported by a crisscross maze of steelwork. Strauss said he could build it for $27 million. The design lacked the simple elegance and beauty of the Golden Gate Bridge that later evolved from his drawing board.

Eleven years passed from the time Strauss's design was made public in December 1923 to the start of construction. This intervening period was one of deep anguish and acrimony. Money to start the bridge would have to come from San Franciscans and the people living in five counties north of the Golden Gate. But residents of these areas were not at all certain they needed or wanted the bridge. Ferry service connecting San Francisco with the north counties at Sausalito

148 / The Golden Gate Bridge

had been operating since 1868, and many people were for keeping the status quo. In addition, the north counties were not heavily populated at that time, and the area was chiefly known for recreation and lumbering. Would the bridge get enough use to return its cost through tolls?

Many doubted that the bridge could be built in this earthquake zone amid swirling waters. They were certain it would go crashing into the Golden Gate, and all their tax dollars with it. Moreover, how could Strauss ever find enough workmen—except those who were bent upon suicide—to build this gigantic bridge while perching hundreds of feet in the air, and constantly buffeted by cold winds from off the Pacific? Fog and the rainy season would make construction highly dangerous. At these dizzying heights, the glare from the water could cause workers to take one misstep which would send them

Illustration (top) shows steel latticework of bridge roadway suspended by vertical steel suspender ropes. Bridge is supported by twin cables, each about 3½ feet in diameter. Lower diagram shows a cross-section of the bridge, near center span, indicating the six roadway lanes and two sidewalks.

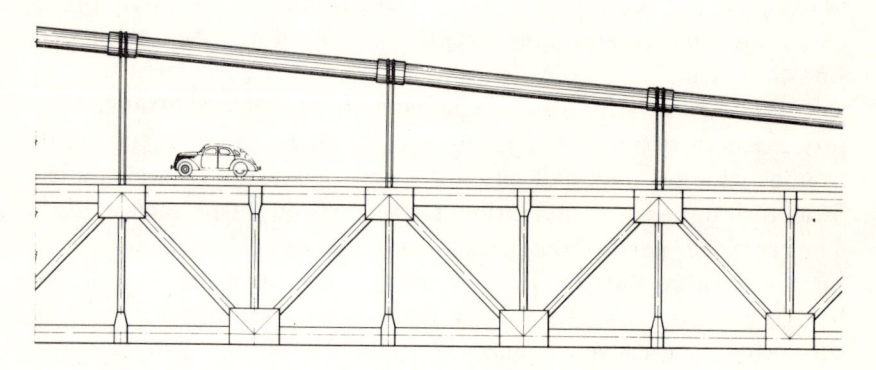

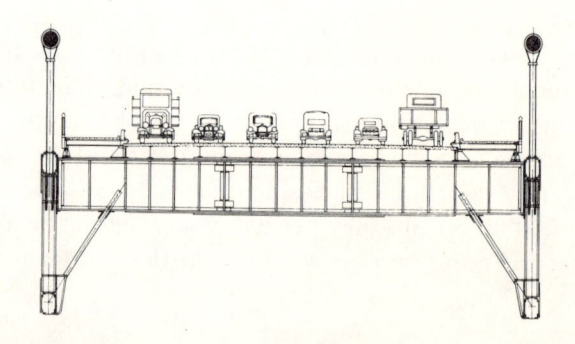

plunging hundreds of feet to certain death in the cold Golden Gate. The generally accepted formula among engineers at that time was that one worker would be killed for each $1 million that a bridge cost. That meant that the Golden Gate Bridge would cost twenty lives. Strauss replied that he would never undertake to build the bridge if he thought it could not be done safely. Not only would he insist that a safety net be strung, but workers would be provided with glare-proof goggles of tinted glass that had been developed for use by Navy gunners. Dieticians would plan meals that prevented lightheadedness. Workers would be carefully watched by supervisors at the start of each shift to ensure their alertness before being allowed to begin. A new type of headgear—common today, but unknown at that time—would be supplied to each worker. It was called a hardhat.

There was much to be said for building the bridge. Businessmen living in the north counties could commute to their San Francisco offices in less than half the time it took them to drive to the ferry and wait their turn to cross. Moreover, the bridge would make the recreational areas more easily accessible, and there would be no more hours of waiting on weekends and holidays while long lines of cars backed up behind the ferry terminals. But the clincher, as far as north county residents were concerned, was the fact that easier access would encourage home-building, causing property values to skyrocket.

Bridge-booster organizations were formed, including the Golden Gate Association. On May 25, 1923, Governor Friend W. Richardson signed the Golden Gate Bridge and Highway District Act, which created a special tax district in the six counties. The district could levy an annual tax of 2.5 cents per $100 of assessed property valuation. The rest of the bridge-building money would come from a bond issue approved by the electorate.

Opposition to the bridge had grown formidable. Critics said Strauss's bridge was ugly—which it was—and would destroy the scenic splendor of the Golden Gate and the surrounding hills. Assuming a bridge could successfully be built—which was at that point very much open to doubt—the cost would be prohibitive. At least one banker said the bridge would be "an economic crime." Lumberers in the forests north of San Francisco did not want any more tourists roaming the redwoods than there were already; somebody might get the idea to preserve the redwoods as recreational parks.

Most steamship lines wanted no part of the Golden Gate Bridge. It was impossible, they claimed, to build a bridge high enough so that their huge ships could pass under it. In these already treacherous waters, they said, the situation should not be worsened by a disaster waiting to happen when a ship in a fog or off course slammed into the bridge while several hundred cars and trucks were passing over it.

For a while it appeared the bridge idea was doomed, especially when the United States War Department reminded everybody that it had supreme jurisdiction over all navigable waters, and its policy was that no bridge be built across the Golden Gate. Its objections were similar to those of the steamship lines, plus one other: In the event of war, enemy bombers could drop the bridge and effectively block the United States Navy fleet at the huge shipyard and drydock at Hunters Point inside the Golden Gate.

Strauss overcame the steamship lines' and the War Department's objections when he convinced them that his bridge would stand higher than any ship afloat or contemplated. There would, moreover, be four foghorns on the bridge. Two, on the San Francisco tower, would blare the traditional stay-away signal. The other two would be mounted in the exact center of the bridge and serve to guide ships along the center of the main channel. Ship captains would later say that the Golden Gate Bridge marks the only channel where they steer toward the sound of foghorns instead of away from them. Nor need the War Department fear that well-placed bombs would block the channel. If that happened, said Strauss, the entire bridge could quickly be dynamited to the bottom of the deep gorge of the Golden Gate.

Even more heat came from the Southern Pacific Railroad. The railroad was a large landowner and would be profoundly affected by the bridge property tax. The SP also owned fifty-one percent of the stock in Golden Gate Ferries, Inc., which had a monopoly on transportation service between San Francisco and the north counties.

In the end, however, it was the popularity of the family automobile which decided that the bridge must be built. With each passing year, traffic jams worsened at the ferry terminals, especially on weekends and holidays, when San Franciscans headed for recreational areas in the north counties. On Memorial Day weekend, 1926, for example, the San Francisco *Examiner* reported that eight thousand homeward-bound automobiles were backed up behind the Sausalito terminal.

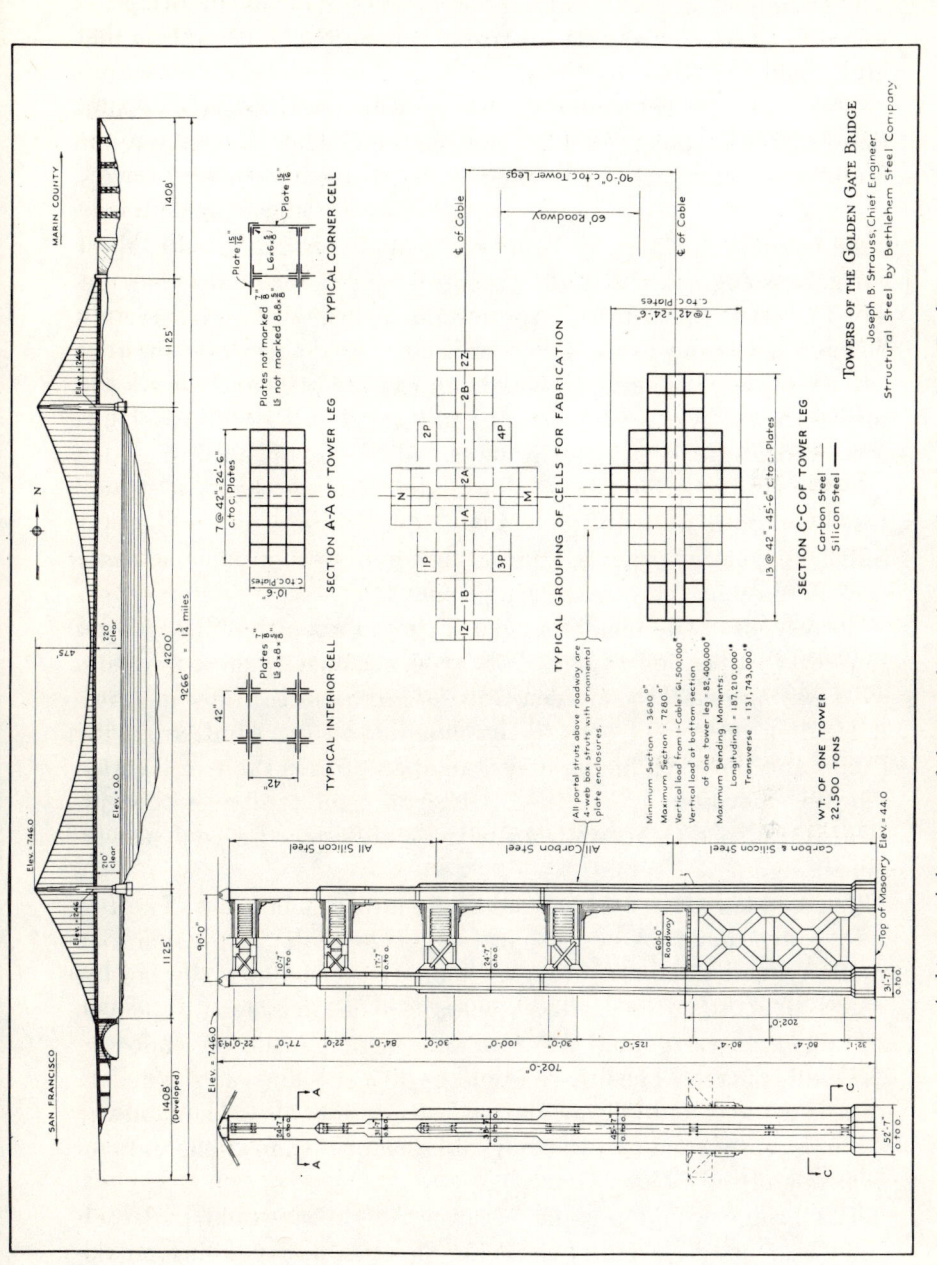

Architectural diagrams of the two identical towers of the Golden Gate Bridge.

The ferries ran all night, but at noon the next day, one thousand automobiles were still waiting to cross. "It was the world's worst traffic glut," said the *Examiner.*

Still there were delays, not the least of which were lingering doubts that firm foundations could be found in the Golden Gate in which to build stout piers that would support the bridge's twin steel towers. On August 22, 1929, Bridge District directors appointed Strauss chief engineer, Clifford E. Paine his assistant, and a board of three consulting engineers to study the problems. A week later they decided to settle the foundations question. A drilling barge made test borings across the strait. The results convinced them that the rock bottom of the Golden Gate would support the piers and towers. On the north side, moreover, borings had located a ledge of bedrock. It was an ideal site for the Marin tower and offered the advantage that the pier could be built in shallow water at lower than anticipated costs. In addition, the offshore site enabled Strauss to lengthen the center suspension span of the bridge and thus provide a wider margin of safety for ships passing under it.

Strauss meanwhile had changed his mind about building a rigid cantilever-suspension bridge. That type was exactly the opposite of what was needed if the Golden Gate was to be successfully spanned. A rigid bridge could very likely collapse. Strong winds from the Pacific and the wide fluctuations of temperatures in the area dictated a bridge that literally breathed. Discarding the cantilever concept, Strauss returned to his drawing board and designed a total suspension bridge.

The Golden Gate Bridge would have three main spans. The two side spans would each be 1,125 feet long. The center suspension span would extend 4,200 feet—longer than any ever built. Including the access structures, the bridge would be 8,981 feet long. The two towers would each stand 746 feet tall on piers made of reinforced steel and concrete. The bridge would be 90 feet wide to accommodate a six-lane concrete highway and pedestrian sidewalks. The roadway was to be suspended by two stout cables embedded in anchorages on each side of the Golden Gate.

The bridge would breathe because the cables would pull each tower as much as twenty-two inches shoreward, depending on the temperature and the weight of traffic. Under the heaviest combinations of loading and extremes of temperatures, the bridge at midspan

The most difficult job in the building of the Golden Gate Bridge was the construction of this pier for the tower support on the San Francisco side.

could rise 10 feet above or ease itself that much below its normal elevation of 220 feet above mean high water. Even if a one-hundred-mile-an-hour gale ripped into the Golden Gate, the bridge would slough it off by swaying only 21 feet at midspan.

Strauss called in architect Irving F. Morrow, who translated the bridge-builder's engineering marvel into a work of art. Morrow designed steel plates to cover and conceal ugly crossbraces normally seen in conventional bridge towers. The Golden Gate Bridge would exude much of its graceful beauty because Morrow made the towers look elegantly taller by gradually tapering them. And Morrow delighted Bay Area motorists and tourists by shedding the traditional solid bridge side rails and replacing them with see-throughs to provide an unforgettable view of San Francisco, the hills north of the city, the Golden Gate, the Pacific Ocean and the San Francisco Bay.

Had any bridge approaching the Golden Gate in total length ever been built? "No," admitted Strauss. Could he build it? Certainly, he said, and at a cost of slightly more than one-third of the $100,000,000 originally expected. On November 4, 1930, a $35-million bond issue proposition to build the bridge was put to voters in the six counties. By a whopping margin of more than three to one they told Strauss to get on with the job. That the proposition carried by such an overwhelming majority was undoubtedly due largely to the Great Depression, into which the United States had just plunged. Building the bridge would mean more jobs for the unemployed.

But enthusiasm was dampened as new roadblocks delayed the start of construction three more years. There were grave doubts that the nation's securities market, caught in the Depression, would buy the bonds, especially while incessant rumors continued that the bridge could never stand in the Golden Gate. To put these stories to rest once and for all, the Bridge District directors voted to reexamine the floor of the Golden Gate with deep-sea divers and to submit their reports and other tests to a board of professional geologists and engineers. Six board members agreed the rock bottom of the Golden Gate had more than adequate strength to support the bridge.

There was but one dissenter to the report. He said the proposed site for the tower on the San Francisco side was of unsafe, flakey rock. On top of that, the story somehow got out that one of the deep-sea divers said the bottom of the Golden Gate was "as soft as plum pudding," and that he had seen mermaid caverns on the very spot on which the San Francisco tower would stand. Critics had a field day. Other divers were sent down to take another look. They explored ten acres around the San Francisco pier site. When they came back up they said they had seen neither plum pudding, nor mermaids. That report tended to quiet the skeptics, but then a new and worse threat arose.

Attorneys representing the Southern Pacific, one of the most powerful corporations in California; a large downtown San Francisco property-holding company; and a huge lumbering corporation in one of the tax-district counties challenged the validity of the Bridge District's authority to levy taxes. They claimed that the taxes were confiscatory and that public funds were being used to put a private corporation—Golden Gate Ferries, Inc.—out of business. They took their case to the California State Supreme Court and to the United States District Court of Appeals.

San Francisco had never seen the like of this battle. While the Southern Pacific and the other companies felt obliged to protect the interests of their shareholders, public opinion was solidly against them. The people needed the jobs that the Golden Gate Bridge would provide. Attacks focused on the Southern Pacific because it was the strongest litigant. Newspaper editorials castigated the railroad. The San Francisco County Council of the American Legion passed a resolution which said, "The opposing interests are acting against the public welfare in withholding employment from needy persons." Scathing nightly radio broadcasts cast the railroad as a villain stealing food from the mouths of children.

One of the Southern Pacific's major sources of revenue was hauling automobiles and related merchandise. On December 2, 1931, William L. Hughson, president of the San Francisco Motor Car Dealers Association, sent telegrams to auto manufacturers and suppliers and told them to route their shipments to the Bay Area via the Santa Fe Railway and other carriers. Dozens of receivers of other freight sent similar requests. Shippers boycotted the Southern Pacific. On August 9, 1932, the railroad capitulated and said it would withdraw its appeal from the earlier Supreme Court ruling which had gone against it. S. P. Eastman, president of the ferry company, fired one last shot: "I still believe that the project is largely a promotion, that a bridge across the Golden Gate is ill-founded and ill-advised and will impose a great burden on taxpayers out of all pro-

156 / The Golden Gate Bridge

portion to benefits." The other litigants soon withdrew their attempts to block the bridge.

Three weeks later, a syndicate including the Bank of America, headquartered in San Francisco, agreed to buy the first $6 million of construction bonds, and the following day, September 2, 1932, the Bridge District directors had the first check for $184,600. Board Chairman A. P. Giannini personally pledged the bank's continuing support, and the remaining $29 million in bonds was taken.

Amid the hostility generated by the battle over the bridge, nobody realized that the railroad and the other opponents had inadvertently saved the bridge-builders a huge sum of money. Soon after the 1930 bond issue passed, the district had called for bids on ten contracts to

Construction work on anchorages and pylons on the San Francisco side of the Golden Gate. The bridgework extends out and over historic Fort Point. Note the trestle leading to the San Francisco pier and tower. Guidelines for the soon-to-be-raised suspension cables can be seen connecting the towers.

build the bridge. The bids had expired, and new ones were called for. On November 4, 1932, Bridge District directors opened the new bids and discovered that contractors, desperate for work during the Depression, had submitted bids which totaled around $600,000 less than the earlier ones.

The major contract—$10,696,562—went to the McClintic-Marshall Corporation, a division of Bethlehem Steel Corporation, which would provide the steel for towers and the superstructure. The cables, suspenders and related accessories would be supplied under a $5,855,000 contract awarded to the John A. Roebling's Sons Company. The Pacific Bridge Company won the $3,325,984 contract to build the Marin and San Francisco piers.

Plans called for work to begin with construction of the bridge-support pylons on each side of the Golden Gate, together with four suspension cable anchorages, two on each side. Then the tower piers would be built. Nobody doubted that the San Francisco pier would be the most difficult part of the entire job, but it was to be far more challenging than anyone expected. Unlike the Marin pier, which would be set in shallow water, the San Francisco pier would be the first one ever to be built in deep ocean waters. After the piers would come erection of the steel towers. The next step was expected to be the most dangerous: stringing the two cables between the anchorages and looping them over the 746-foot-high towers. That done, the roadway spans would be built. Nobody had the slightest inkling that what was expected to be a fairly routine roadway construction would turn out to be the deadliest part of the job.

Work started on January 5, 1933, when a pair of steam shovels began anchorage excavations at Lime Point. These were to be no ordinary holes filled with concrete. An unprecedented amount of strength would be required to anchor securely the 24,500-ton cables to prevent their enormous weight and pull from causing the anchorages to slide into the Golden Gate. The anchorages were built in three interlocking blocks. The bottom block extended deep into bedrock which was cut away to form a sawtoothlike profile along the base. The anchor block, also built with sawteeth for interfacing with the base block to further prevent slippage, was poured next. Attached to it were girders secured to the rear of the anchor block. Sixty-one sets of chains extended 130 feet through the concrete and ended in links. Strands of cables would be threaded through them.

On top of the base and anchor block was poured a massive weight block which also fit tongue-in-groove. When done, the anchorages on each side of the Golden Gate would weigh 240 million pounds.

San Franciscans celebrated the start of work on the bridge on February 26, 1933, with a parade and the ceremonial turning of a shovelful of earth while airplanes laid a symbolic smokescreen across the Golden Gate where the bridge would stand. The crush of people was so great that ceremonies had to be cut short. It was a matter of civic pride, but also a realization that jobs were available again. Except for certain specialists, hiring was restricted to those who had been residents of the six counties for at least one year. Pay scales for the hundreds who would be employed ranged from $5.50 a day for laborers to $11 daily for structural ironworkers. (Strangely, only a relatively small crowd showed up five months later when the three-year construction work began on the smaller San Francisco-Oakland Bay Bridge, where a larger workforce would be hired.)

In Pennsylvania, meanwhile, fabrication of steelwork began at Bethlehem's Pottstown and Steelton plants. Starting in March 1933, large prefabricated sections of the towers were loaded on railroad cars, taken to the Philadelphia docks, loaded aboard Bethlehem ships and taken through the Panama Canal to McClintic-Marshall's storage yards at Alameda, five miles from the bridge site. From there they would be barged as needed to the bridge. That August, Bethlehem shipped gigantic derricks to Alameda, where they stood ready to begin lifting steel into place as soon as the Marin pier was done.

The Marin pier was started first, and work proceeded rapidly. A U-shaped cofferdam to keep out water was fitted against a cliff at the end of Lime Point. When the cofferdam was done and water pumped out, steam shovels scooped out a 64-foot-deep hole, 80 feet wide and 160 feet long at the bottom. Concrete came in by barge and by a new kind of truck—cement mixers. These rotary cement haulers are common today, but they were a novelty to those who saw them shuttling between the mixing plant and the pier site, where the cement was poured into the hole through chutes the workers called elephant trunks. Marin pier cement was supplied by a batching plant in a nearby cove. A similar mixing plant was built on the San Francisco side near the Presidio. The aggregate that was mixed into the cement was drawn from centuries of deposits of oyster shells. When finished late in June 1933, the pier stood 44 feet above water and resembled a loaf of bread. The 45,000-ton pier cost $436,000 — a pittance compared to the already started San Francisco pier, which could cost more than six times that.

The site for the San Francisco pier was 1,100 feet offshore in open sea, where swift tides ran more than seven miles an hour. There was no protection against fierce winds or ocean storms that regularly sent gigantic waves churning into the Golden Gate. Because the tides reversed themselves four times a day, there was about a twenty-minute interval between them when the water was relatively calm. Only during those periods was it safe for deep-sea divers to descend to the floor of the Golden Gate. Under these conditions, it would be extremely difficult and slow going to anchor the pier supports to bedrock.

Pacific Bridge planned to use divers, creeper derricks and a derrick barge to do the job by first building around the pier site a protective fender the shape and size of a football field. This fender would be set 65 feet into bedrock and consist of twenty-two interlocking stacks of steel boxes, each more than 2 feet wide, and filled with concrete. Just before the ends of the fender looped around for joining, a gigantic steel caisson would be floated through the opening and sunk to provide a platform on which to build the pier. Then the fender wall would be completed, the water pumped out, and the pier built on top of the caisson from bedrock foundations as deep as 110 feet. It looked easy on paper. In reality it was doomed.

The first hint of trouble ahead came after a 1,100-foot-long trestle to carry men, material and derricks out to the pier site was finished on August 1, 1933. Exactly two weeks later, after a heavy fog had settled over the Golden Gate, an outbound freighter, the *Sidney M. Hauptman*, was shoved far off course by vicious ebbtides. The McCormick Lines steamship slammed into the trestle and tore out more than 120 feet of it. The trestle was rebuilt, and work began again.

The fender and pier excavations were done from aboard the steam-powered derrick barge *Ajax*. Long pipes were lowered overboard until they were a few feet from the bottom. Fitted inside was a pencil-shaped steel shaft with a two-foot-long point. The solid shaft, weighing 5,000 pounds, was repeatedly dropped down the tube until a two-foot-deep hole was punched.

The pencil-shaft was then removed, and a thirty-inch bomb containing three pounds of dynamite was lowered into the hole and deto-

Work proceeds as support wires are stretched across the Golden Gate preparatory to spinning the stout suspension cables.

nated. About fifteen bombs per hole resulted in an eighteen-foot-deep crater. When six of these craters were dynamited, the *Ajax* lowered another bomb into each. These bigger bombs were twenty feet long and were loaded with two hundred pounds of dynamite. When six bombs were tapped into place, the *Ajax* backed off to a safe distance, and the bombs were detonated. Fountains of water spewed high, and, until they became accustomed to them, San Franciscans thought the shocks were earthquakes.

The *Ajax* steamed back over the site and used dredger buckets to scoop out the broken rock, which was loaded into barges for dumping at sea. Aside from the dangers of working with dynamite, there were many unpleasant days aboard the *Ajax*. Eight-foot swells often set the barge tossing, and seasoned crewmen were seasick.

On October 31, 1933, the first five fender sections were in place. That day, a fierce Pacific storm sent high waves into the Golden Gate. Three of the five fenders were washed away, and the end of the trestle and much equipment were wrecked. The Pacific Bridge Company started again, only to have their work demolished once more starting December 13, when a two-day gale sent waves as high as two-story buildings crashing into the Golden Gate. Eight hundred feet of trestle was torn out.

Strauss had even more bad news for the Bridge District directors. The excavation blastings had shattered so much rock that the fender foundations, to get a firm footing, would have to be sunk another 65 feet into bedrock, instead of the 35 feet originally planned. To blast a 110-foot-deep basin as big as a football field would jack up costs another $350,000 and put the bridge nearly a year behind schedule. These setbacks angered the builders, but they also made them more determined than ever that the Golden Gate would not defeat them. They were, moreover, encouraged by the sight of the steadily rising Marin tower, which stood 500 feet tall and would be completed in six months.

A new and stronger trestle was built, blasting continued, and two creeper derricks, working from the left and right sides of the trestle, lowered stacks of fender sections, which were secured by deep-sea divers. When the fender was eight shy of the twenty-two stacks needed to enclose the pier side, the caisson was floated in. On October 8, 1934, three tugs pulled it from a nearby Oakland shipyard where it was built. The four-story-tall caisson was eased through the opening and moored, preparatory to lowering it to the bottom by filling it with concrete.

The following day the Golden Gate showed its treachery again. A storm sent gigantic swells swarming into the strait and the open fender wall. The 10,800-ton caisson, bobbing like a cork, snapped its moorings and began to batter the sides of the fender. By midnight, Strauss and Pacific Bridge officials decided that unless the caisson was removed, disaster would surely result. Three things could happen: the caisson could smash itself while pounding against the fender; it could sink, with equally costly results; or it could wreck the fender wall. The caisson was tugged out of the fender and later hauled to sea, where the piece of junk that had cost $300,000 was sent to the bottom. Instead of a caisson, the San Francisco pier would be built on steel-reinforced concrete.

Completion of the fender was rushed day and night. On October 28, 1934, the twin derricks enclosed the pier site with fender sections standing fifteen of the eventual forty-four feet above water. Victory at last. The water inside the fender was calm. While deep-sea divers attached forms to ensure tightness, rotary cement trucks rushed back

Cable-spinning devices shuttle across the Golden Gate while laying the lead-pencil-thick wires of the suspension cables. The three-wheelers zoomed more than 600 feet a minute and often laid 1,000 miles of wire during an eight-hour working day.

and forth from the batching plant with concrete which was poured to form solid steel-and-concrete boxes. Returning to the surface, the divers told of hundreds of fish swimming inside the fender, including small sharks and an octopus. San Francisco newspapers described it as the world's largest fishbowl.

Meanwhile, pumps drained the aquarium of more than five million gallons of water preparatory to continuing with the cement foundations for the pier itself. The San Francisco pier was at last done on January 8, 1935, nearly two years after it was started. Philip Hart, president of Pacific Bridge, said, "This was one of the most difficult and hazardous pieces of construction work ever attempted." Nobody disputed him.

Construction of the San Francisco tower started two days later. It would be identical to the Marin tower and similarly built. Grinders flattened the top of the pier to a tolerance of one thirty-second inch to ensure that the tower would stand straight and true. More than one hundred steel rods were embedded fifty-three feet in the concrete, and five-inch steel slabs were welded and riveted to them to form the tower base.

The creeper derrick that had built the Marin tower was floated to the San Francisco pier and mounted on the base. Prefabricated tower sections were barged five miles from the Alameda warehouse and lifted into place, welded and riveted. The tower would consist of two legs, ninety feet apart. They would be assembled by a building-block system of steadily decreasing numbers of cells: ninety-seven at the base of each leg, and twenty-one at the top. They would be connected by six supporting crossbraces.

The stacks of cells grew steadily taller. Using each leg for support, the derrick crept, spiderlike, up the legs and began hoisting more cells into place. Red-hot rivets shot up pneumatic tubes to riveters who, wearing miner's lamps in the darkness inside the cells, gunned them into place. Some 600,000 rivets went into the towers as the creeper derrick edged up the legs forty feet at a time while the staccato of the riveting sounded like machine-gun fire. The tower gradually formed a beehive of more than five thousand cells, a labyrinth of dark passageways inside, connected by twenty-three miles of ladders. Occasionally a worker got lost. That problem was solved when a twenty-three-page instruction booklet showed them how to get in and out.

The tower was topped off when the derrick lifted three enormous steel castings weighing a total of 150 tons. These castings, when bolted together, formed two grooved saddles for the suspension cables. On June 28, 1935, the last of the steelwork was lifted into place, and the 746-foot-tall twin of the Marin tower cast its silhouette on the shimmering waters of the Golden Gate. The towers were taller than any San Francisco building, and there were no higher manmade structures between San Francisco and New York.

Erection of the suspension cables, the job that everybody considered the most dangerous part of building the Golden Gate Bridge, began at dawn, August 2, 1935, after the Coast Guard had closed the strait to all shipping. Thick fog blanketed the Golden Gate as a barge began feeling its way across from Lime Point while unreeling a thick wire cable to support the first of two construction catwalks that would drape the length of the bridge. The crossing to the San Francisco pier took an hour.

At noon, derricks on top of the towers hooked onto the rope and

Looking from the San Francisco side, we can see the catwalks nearing completion with the placement of steel truss crosswalks.

lifted it to just under the suspension cable saddles, where workers secured it. Twenty-five more ropes were similarly laid, hoisted, and fastened. Vertical support cables were clamped to these ropes. Next, steel mesh and redwood planking for the catwalk flooring was attached to the ends of these support cables. The catwalks, about 16 feet wide, hung 3 feet under the contour the suspension cables would take. Steel truss crosswalks were built at about 500-foot intervals between the catwalks. Added strength to prevent the catwalks from violently swaying in the relentless winds was provided by a tower-supported network of storm cables. The catwalks were finished on September 27. The stringing of the two suspension cables could begin.

    Strauss designed what many people believe to be the most beautiful bridge in the world. But it could not have been built except for the genius of a German-born immigrant, John A. Roebling. He had devised a spinning-wheel system for stringing suspension cables across bridges by using devices that looked like three-wheel bicycles. Founding a cable company in Trenton, New Jersey, Roebling had successfully strung cables for the Niagara Falls Suspension Bridge, among others. But he was most famous for the suspension cables that held up the Brooklyn Bridge, although he never lived to see it finished. Roebling suffered fatal injuries while working on the Brooklyn Bridge, and his oldest son took over the business.

Roebling workers strung guide wires for the cables, and also strung ropes for pulling the spinning devices between the anchorages of the Golden Gate Bridge. Coils of pencil-thick cable arrived from Trenton and were mounted, forty at a time, on reels at each side of the Golden Gate. Spinning started November 12, 1935, and provided a sight San Franciscans would never forget. Hooking onto strands of wire feeding from the reels, each three-wheeler spectacularly zoomed more than 600 feet a minute to the top of the tower on its side, crossed over the saddle, and roller-coastered down to meet—in the middle of the bridge—the other three-wheeler coming from the opposite shore. The strands were automatically exchanged, and the spinners continued their race to the other side while playing out six

Workers on scaffolding erect roadway supports suspended from the cables. Note the safety net under them. The nineteen who were saved by the net formed The Half Way To Hell Club.

wires with each passage. The wires were fastened to the anchorages and tightened to specifications.

Workers on the catwalks, which swayed as much as eight feet in stiff winds, made sure the spinners stayed on course. Sometimes the workers had to crawl on top of the cable to free the strands when the machines jammed. The spinners operated so swiftly that one thousand miles of wire were often laid during an eight-hour workday. Each night, when the cables cooled to a uniform temperature, surveying instruments precisely adjusted the guide wires to prepare for the following day's spinning and to ensure the desired 465-foot center sag, which would dip to about five feet off the roadway.

The wires were spliced with steel sleeves which made the joints stronger than the wires themselves. Spinning was completed on May 20, 1936. Each cable was 7,650 feet long and contained 27,572 parallel wires grouped into sixty-one strands hooked to the anchorages. The total length of wire spun was eighty thousand miles—enough to go around the earth three times at the Equator. Enormous pressure was applied along the entire length of the 5-foot-thick cables to compact them. The cables were then bound with steel bands and wrapped with galvanized wire to protect them against the elements. Each cable is about 3-1/2 feet in diameter. The work was completed without the loss of a single life and with only four injuries.

On June 18, 1936, work began on the 4,200-foot center suspension span, the longest in the world. (The Golden Gate Bridge held that record until the Verrazano-Narrows Bridge, with its 4,260-foot-long main suspension span, connected Brooklyn and Staten Island in 1964.) Prefabricated steel sandwiches, 25 feet long, were carried by barge to each tower. To equalize the load on the towers, the shoreward spans were built simultaneously. The spans were connected to the suspension cables at 50-foot intervals by vertical steel suspender ropes that were nearly three inches thick.

Although there were some who said that the safety record so far made it a waste of $130,000, Strauss insisted on stretching a safety net of manila rope under the entire length of the bridge. The net hung about thirty feet below the bridgework and ten feet out from each side. It was extended before each new section was started. Before the bridge was done, nineteen workers whose lives were saved when they fell into the net formed a social organization which they called The Half Way To Hell Club. Kermit Moore, twenty-three, was not so lucky. On October 21, 1936, a derrick toppled on the Marin shore span, and Moore was killed instantly under its crushing weight. He was the first, but not the last, to be killed while building the Golden Gate Bridge.

The steel roadway was all but completed on November 18, 1936. During a brief ceremony, Strauss himself took the controls of a traveler derrick and lowered the steelwork into place. There remained another six months of work. The roadway had to be concreted, the sidewalks laid, the see-through railings installed, and the bridge painted international orange. Those months did not pass without incident. On January 26, 1937, a locomotive pulling carloads of cement lost its brakes. The engineer jumped to safety as the runaway train left the tracks. The engine plunged fifteen feet and hit the Marin anchorage. To this day, the myth persists that there is a railroad locomotive buried in the Golden Gate Bridge.

Work was rapidly nearing an end on February 17, 1937, when a

To equalize the load on the towers, the shoreward spans were simultaneously built out from opposite sides. This view looks toward the Marin County side and shows the San Francisco work-trestle at the left.

horror was forever etched in the memories of the builders of the Golden Gate Bridge. Workers were on a scaffold under the roadway near the exact center of the bridge when one of the support hangers spread open. The ten-ton scaffold broke off and fell into the net, which could not support that much weight. Snapping ropes sounded like gunfire, and a trembling later described by workers as similar to an earthquake rippled across the bridge, as the victims plunged into the Golden Gate.

One body was recovered almost immediately, and the scaffold bobbed to the surface in several hours. Two days later searchers with grappling hooks grabbed onto the net, which Golden Gate tides had carried out to sea. Inside it were nine bodies. The names of the eleven workers who were killed while building the Golden Gate Bridge were engraved in a bronze plaque that is embedded in concrete above the sidewalk on the ocean side of the bridge.

Strauss forbade further work until a new net was completed on April 2. The steelwork was done twenty-five days later when the final rivet—solid gold and weighing one pound—was driven home by Edwin Stanley, the man who had put in the first steel one. Some 83,000 tons of structural steel, 24,500 tons of cables, suspenders and other steelwork, plus 389,000 cubic yards of concrete had gone into the bridge. A week-long community fiesta began on May 26, 1937, to celebrate the completion of the bridge. The following day the bridge was opened to pedestrians, and 200,000 of them paid a nickel apiece to walk across it, picnic on it, and dance on the roadway, while marveling at the breathtaking view.

The Golden Gate Bridge was to become synonynous with San Francisco. It has often been described as the Statue of Liberty of the Pacific Coast. In a 1975 poll, the United States Department of Commerce asked travel-industry representatives which construction had the greatest tourist appeal. The Golden Gate Bridge ranked first, followed by the Mount Rushmore National Memorial in South Dakota. Tragically, the lofty Golden Gate has become a magnet for emotionally disturbed people. By 1976 at least 561 people had committed suicide by leaping from the bridge, and officials suspect that there are others whose suicides have gone by unwitnessed, their bodies carried out to sea. Only seven have survived the plunge.

The Golden Gate Bridge, opened to traffic on May 28, 1937, has an annual capacity of seventy million cars and six million trucks. On

July 1, 1971, the $35 million construction bonds were paid off. Strauss did not live to enjoy that satisfaction; he died seven months after the bridge was finished. San Francisco Bay residents with a flair for history recall that Strauss had said shortly before his death: "The bridge which 'could not be' and which 'should not be,' which the War Department would not permit, which the rocky ledge under the pier base would not support, which would have no traffic and which would ruin the beauty of the Golden Gate, stands before you in all its majestic splendor—in complete refutation of every attack upon it."

X

The Gateway Arch

THE SIMPLE, graceful elegance of the Gateway Arch in St. Louis hides the fact that the builders of America's tallest monument had to overcome extraordinary challenges before they completed it. The colossal arch casting its shadow on the Mississippi River is a memorial to Thomas Jefferson and the pioneers who opened up the West for exploration and settlement.

But the steel-and-concrete arch also is a testimonial to its builders, who used tools as old as hammers and shovels and as new as computers and gamma-radiation cameras as they braved dangers while perching hundreds of feet in the air as strong winds buffeting the legs set the working platforms to swaying. Before they started the job, it was expected that many would plunge to their deaths. Not one worker was killed, but that is only part of the fascinating story of how they built the Gateway Arch.

The idea for the memorial started in 1933 with Mayor Bernard F. Dickman of St. Louis and several civic leaders, including Luther Ely Smith, who later became mayor. Smith's vigorous support earned him the nickname "Father of the Memorial." These men recalled that Meriwether Lewis and William Clark had set out from St. Louis in 1804 on their famous expedition to explore the Northwest Territory shortly after President Thomas Jefferson concluded the Louisiana Purchase Treaty with France in 1803. The Louisiana Purchase added more than 800,000 square miles to the newly independent United States and doubled the size of the nation. St. Louis, near the con-

The completed Gateway Arch, with Mississippi riverboats in the foreground. The 630-foot-high arch frames St. Louis's Old Courthouse, where Dred Scott's right to be a free man was first pleaded.

fluence of the Mississippi and Missouri rivers, was a village founded in 1764 by French fur traders. During the years following the Louisiana Purchase, St. Louis became the gateway through which countless hundreds of thousands of people trekked westward to settle and expand the American frontier.

In 1935 the Jefferson National Expansion Memorial Association was organized in St. Louis by the civic leaders. The city and the Federal government agreed to build a $30 million national monument on the riverfront, with St. Louis paying part of the cost. President Franklin D. Roosevelt signed an executive order placing the memorial under the jurisdiction of the United States Department of the Interior.

As has been demonstrated time and time again, the story of the construction of national memorials in the United States usually is one of long delays from concept to creation. The Jefferson National Expansion Memorial was no exception. Although the Federal government and the City of St. Louis had agreed in principle that the project should be done, annual money bills had to be debated in Congress, where there were other demands on the Federal budget. The St. Louis electorate, moreover, had to approve a bond issue to raise money for it. Still more delays would result because of the site chosen: a rectangular area of about thirty-six blocks immediately west of the downtown levee along the Mississippi. The area was blighted with decaying structures, many of them tall brick buildings. It would take years for condemnation proceedings, demolition, and clearing away of the rubble. Then, tracks of an industrial railroad would have to be relocated in an underground tunnel that would have to be built.

By 1947 fund-raising had progressed to the point where the Association sponsored a national competition for a design for the memorial. The entry of Eero Saarinen, thirty-seven, an innovative architect known for his brilliant adaptation of domes in his structures, won the $50,000 prize over two hundred other entries. Saarinen, a native of Finland, never saw the arch; he died in 1961 before it was started. In addition to the Gateway Arch, Saarinen left behind a notable body of work, including the Trans World Airlines terminal at New York's Idlewild (now Kennedy) International Airport; Dulles International Airport near Washington, D.C.; and the Columbia Broadcasting Building in New York.

Like gigantic insects, creeper derricks move up the outside legs of the Gateway Arch as they lift more triangular sections into place.

Saarinen's design for the arch was the essence of simplicity. Placed parallel to the Mississippi River, it ideally fit the concept of St. Louis as the nation's historic gateway for westward expansion. The arch would dominate the park; the rest of the memorial, consisting of a visitor center and a museum, would be built underground. From a technical viewpoint, the arch design was known as a catenary curve—the shape a chain takes when suspended between two points of support. Saarinen merely turned the catenary curve upside down, and—presto—the Gateway Arch.

The legs would stand 630 feet apart and curve to a height of 630 feet. By comparison with other national monuments, it would be 75 feet taller than the Washington Monument and 335 feet taller than the Statue of Liberty. The arch would be as tall as a sixty-two-story skyscraper—taller than any building in St. Louis—and longer at the base than two football fields. Built of steel set in a concrete foundation up to the 300-foot level in each leg, the Gateway Arch would weigh 17,246 tons—more than an aircraft carrier—and cost $8 million. Although the arch might look frail, it would be so sturdy as to withstand a 150-mile-an-hour wind and sway no more than eighteen inches.

The arch would consist of 142 triangular-shaped sections of various sizes. The largest would be placed at the bottom of the arch, and the others would slowly taper to the smallest at the top. All sections would be sheathed on the outside with stainless steel plates. Both legs of the arch would be built concurrently as the triangular sections were lifted and placed and welded like building blocks—one atop the other—as the legs gradually curved inward until they joined. The completed arch and its welded joints would be smoothed to make the structure appear to be one continuous loop of stainless steel.

On paper, the Gateway Arch looked simple enough to build. Exactly the opposite was true. The job would require engineering and construction expertise that was without parallel. Skeptics said there was no way it could be built. In the first place, no similar arch of this magnitude or weight had been built anywhere in the world, so there was no previous knowledge on which to draw. At 630 feet, the structure would be too tall for conventional scaffolding for workers. Each leg would have to be self-supporting and bear the additional burden of more than eighty tons of equipment and workers. The Leaning Tower of Pisa had been standing for centuries, but it was only 180 feet high and fourteen feet off the vertical plane. The Gateway Arch builders were proposing to build two towers that would lean more than 300 feet off center before they were joined at 630 feet.

But the most compelling argument concerned the allowable margin of error—only one sixty-fourth inch. How could the builders possibly start from two points 630 feet apart and meet precisely at 630 feet in the sky? It was impossible to do, said the critics, who noted that St. Louis would very likely end up with the dubious distinction of twin leaning towers. All these problems were rather easily solved by the ingenuity of the arch's builders, but we get ahead of our story.

A worse fear was the extreme danger which progressively multiplied the higher the building progressed. The job certainly was not for anybody afraid of heights, small work areas, swaying, or stiff winds. With no protection against the wind, the legs would sway constantly. Would an unusually strong wind set up a back-and-forth vibration and an unstoppable rocking that would send the legs crash-

(Left) Two sections are hoisted simultaneously—a rarity—from railroad cars to their places atop the rapidly rising legs. (Right) Tracks carry the creeper derricks high up the legs.

ing down? The dangers would further be compounded by wintertime snow and ice that would make footing treacherous on a working surface already burdened with construction equipment, workers and building materials. How on earth could the legs withstand all of these things without falling over and carrying the workers to their deaths? Engineering calculations estimated that at least thirteen workers would be killed before the arch was done.

These problems only seemed to whet the enthusiasm of the builders, who were certain they could solve all of them. By 1959 there was sufficient money to start, and a contract was awarded to the MacDonald Construction Company of St. Louis, which assigned the job to one of their best engineers, Art Pritchard, thirty-two, whose experience included building of missile sites. By then the site had been cleared, and Pritchard's most immediate job was to relocate the railroad tracks and to build a supply track from the main line to the worksite. The triangular-shaped sandwich sections for the arch would be fabricated in Pennsylvania and brought by rail directly to the foundations for the legs.

While this work proceeded, test drillings were made to locate solid bedrock for the foundations. In March 1962 MacDonald received another contract: this one for $11,442,418 to build the arch and the underground visitor center. By the following June, excavations had opened foundation holes sixty feet below ground level and thirty feet into bedrock. Concrete for the foundations began to be poured on June 21.

In Pittsburgh, meanwhile, work on the pyramid sections began in the fabrication shops of the Pittsburgh-Des Moines Steel Company (PDM), subcontractors to MacDonald. PDM's Ken Kolkmeier, twenty-seven, another missile-site builder, was put in charge. During the next three years, steel fabricators would weld and bolt together 142 triangular-shaped steel sandwiches from metals supplied by the United States Steel Corporation and other mills.

The largest sandwiches, those for the base of the legs, were made first. The outside of the sandwich consisted of one-quarter-inch-thick stainless steel plates. The center of the sandwich was a smaller triangle made of three-eighth-inch-thick carbon steel. The inner and outer triangles were joined by a network of steel stiffeners, reinforcing rods, and tensioning bolts to make each unit self-supporting. By adapting stressed steel skin design techniques used in aircraft manufacturing, massive interior framework was avoided. The result was lighter weight, plus enormous strength and lean lines that made each sandwich esthetically appealing.

When done, each of these jumbo sandwiches weighed fifteen tons, had fifty-four-foot sides, and stood twelve feet tall. Similar thicknesses of steel and supporting pieces were used in the other sandwiches, including the smallest—those for the top of the arch. The top sections had seventeen-foot sides and stood eight feet tall. Cranes lifted the first pieces onto railroad cars for shipment to St. Louis.

By the time construction was completed, more than 900 tons of stainless steel would be used for the outside walls of the arch—more than for any other construction project. The American Iron & Steel Institute of Washington, D.C., calculated that a total of 5,119 tons of steel plates, stiffeners, reinforcing bars and other metals went into the Gateway Arch, plus 12,127 tons of concrete.

In St. Louis on February 13, 1963, a huge crane lifted the first sandwich from a railroad car and gently set it onto the concrete foundation for the south leg. After measuring instruments confirmed its precise location in the master plan, the steel triangle was firmly anchored by steel splices set into the foundation.

As they would do with all of the other sandwiches, X-ray technicians double-checked the strength of each weld after the long journey from Pennsylvania and the lifting strains put on the joints. One of the radiologists crawled inside the sandwich and taped industrial X-ray film against the welds, while another radiologist readied a gamma-radiation camera outside. They communicated with each other by hammer taps against the steel. When all was ready, the inside radiologist climbed out to avoid exposure to gamma rays. The camera then sent penetrating rays through the steel sandwich and projected the results on film.

Still more strength was ensured as seventy tons of pulling pressure was applied to firmly stretch the steel tendons spliced to those set into the concrete foundations. The tendons in the sandwich would, in turn, be spliced to those inside the sandwich above it. This splicing would continue until the arch was done to form mighty, unbroken bands of taut steel strength from the top of the arch to deep into the foundations. Concrete pouring began when the engineers were satisfied with the welds and the splices. Cranes lifted huge bucketfuls of cement, which was poured into the space between the inner and the outer walls of the sandwich, while workers spread the cement with shovels and other tools.

By August 1, 1963, each leg had a stack of six leaning sandwiches, welded, spliced, and filled with concrete. Workers were starting to sense the winds that created a gentle swaying in the legs, a situation which would become more pronounced the higher up they built. When the legs stood at seventy-two feet, the ground cranes could reach no higher. Kolkmeier supervised the attachment of sets of I-beam railroad tracks to the outer side of each leg and ordered in a pair of PDM's monster-sized creeper derricks, which, for the next several years, would provide some of the most spectacular sights an amateur sidewalk-superintendent of construction could every hope to see.

The brilliant red, white and blue derricks had towering booms and long, telescoping struts for legs that angled inward from the rear of a large work platform and house. Wheels on the legs were fitted to the tracks, and thousands of spectators were treated to the sight of these grotesque, long-legged spiders creeping up the outside legs of the arch. When the creeper derricks reached the desired working height, leveling devices and the telescoping leg struts were adjusted to fit the creepers to the curvature of the arch. Large steel pins anchored the derricks, and the job of lifting more sandwiches and concrete continued.

The legs were too heavy to stand alone as they arched sharply inward above the 500-foot level. Support was provided by a sixty-ton stabilizing strut of crisscrossing steelwork.

Cages lifted the workers to the 43- by 42-foot platforms, where there was everything they needed during the day: tools, welding equipment, a heated lunchroom, bathrooms, a first-aid station, two-way radio equipment for communicating with workers on the ground, and a closed circuit television system to enable the crane operator to see working areas which were otherwise blocked from his vision.

When four more sandwiches were done, the creeper derricks lifted more I-beams, which were attached to the legs. The derricks crept up the railroad, and work began on another four sections. By the fall of 1963, the leaning towers of St. Louis were so tall they were casting their shadows on the Mississippi.

How could the builders be certain they were not deviating from the one-sixty-fourth-inch margin of error? They answered that question each night when the steel had cooled and there were uniform surface temperatures on the legs. Target lights were mounted at the corners of the legs, and sighting instruments were focused on them. The geometric readings taken were fed into a computer, which compared the measurements with the computerized ideal. Any deviation was quickly corrected.

Knowing they were precisely on target, workers continued, one sandwich at a time, the steady process of lifting, fitting, welding, splicing, concrete pouring and smoothing. Echoing across the working platforms was the constant clanking of metal against metal, the piercing shrieks of power-grinders smoothing the surface, the sloshing of cement, the whine of the derrick cable drums and the constant crackling of radio messages between workers on the ground and those hundreds of feet in the air. And, of course, there was the incessant whistling of the wind and the constant swaying.

Work continued during bitterly cold weather. It sometimes became necessary to heat a sandwich to ensure a good bond when cement was poured. The sandwich was wrapped with insulating material while propane-powered heaters warmed it all night and the next morning until the sandwich was ready to be filled with concrete that afternoon.

The number of workers peaked during the 1963-1964 working season to around 250, most of them cement workers. By June 1964 the 300-foot level was reached. From deep in solid bedrock, two sturdy columns of reinforced steel and concrete arched to the 300-foot level. The cement workers' job was over. From here on up—330 more feet—it was mainly up to the steelworkers to complete the arch.

The creeper derricks advanced again and again. When they reached the 400-foot level later in 1964, the nature of the job had changed, and everyone sensed it more than ever. They were doing the same work as they had below, but with the greater height, the swaying became more pronounced, and the biting wind was a constant annoyance. A wind gauge told the workers when it was safe to lift another sandwich. Winds of over thirty miles per hour were considered dangerous, and work stopped until they abated. One day an eighty-four-mile-an-hour wind from off the western prairies buffeted the arch. If you had a queasy stomach, the creeper derricks were not choice places to spend a working day.

On another day, the gauge showed winds well within the safety range. A creeper derrick lowered its hook and began lifting a sand-

After the supporting strut was in place, work continued in a near-horizontal fashion. Dangers increased substantially, and a net was strung between the curving legs. To get a perspective of the height, note the tiny riverboats and autos on the ground below.

wich. When it was almost ready to be swung into place, the wind suddenly shifted, and gusts sent the gauge far beyond the safety margin. If they tried to lift the sandwich over the opening and settle it in place, the wind would likely send it sailing off into space like a steel kite and rip the creeper derrick off, too. The whirring gears of the derrick were stopped, and the sandwich hung suspended, with the leeward side of the leg protecting it from slamming against the arch. When the wind spent itself and it was safe to proceed, the sandwich was lifted into place on a day that would not soon be forgotten.

Sandwiches were now stacked well past the 500-foot level and were arching sharply inward. The legs were now too heavy to stand alone. Support was provided by a sixty-ton stabilizing strut consisting of a crisscrossing network of steelwork. It was lifted on June 17, 1965, and attached to each leg just above the 500-foot level. Workers who had almost grown accustomed to the swaying were surprised. "It doesn't shake and jump up here as much as it used to," one of them radioed a co-worker on the ground.

The derricks crept still higher and anchored for the final time when they were just short of the 600-foot level. What used to be a short climb to work now became a twelve-minute elevator ride to the derrick platform, where, on a clear day, workers could see for at least thirty miles in every direction. From that narrow, dizzying height, automobiles below looked like ants, and large riverboats in the Mississippi were mere slivers.

A large net was strung between the legs, but most workers considered it of doubtful effectiveness if they should fall. Not a few were heard to shrug off the net as a publicity stunt to make people think that dangers were nonexistent and to remind the workers of safety. They needed no reminding. "I wouldn't want to fall in that net," said one of them. "It would be like a trapeze artist falling into a circus net and bouncing right out." Nobody fell into the net to prove whether he was right or wrong, but the workers were more than a little bit impressed when wind blew several of their hardhat helmets into it. The helmets bounced and quickly went soaring off into space.

On October 7, 1965, the first of eight sections with windows was lifted into place, and the workers realized all the more how close they were to completing the arch. Much work remained even after the last sandwich was eased into place. The creeper derricks would slowly back down the legs and lift off the tracks above them while workers filled holes left by the rails and did final polishing.

After the arch was done, passenger trains remained to be built—one in each leg. They would carry visitors from underground entrances in capsule cars as the trains curved upward, ferris-wheel style, to the observation deck. A stairway of 1,076 steps to the deck also had to be built. From the observation room the visitors would be able to look through sixteen windows on each side—on the east side, to see the land from which the westward-bound settlers had come, and on the west side, to view the panoramic challenge of open space and opportunity that had awaited the pioneers.

There was still the visitor center to be built, and an underground Museum of Westward Expansion. The museum, finished in July 1976 and dedicated during the United States Bicentennial celebration, presents the story of westward expansion from various viewpoints: Indians, mountainmen, traders, explorers, soldiers, miners, statesmen, farmers, cattlemen, town and railroad builders.

But all thoughts of the work remaining were put aside on Thursday morning, October 28, 1965, when a huge crowd gathered to watch while the final section was readied for lifting and slipping into place. It was a clear day. The temperature was forty degrees and rising rapidly. Motorists double- and triple-parked along the levee. A band played martial music, and a small fleet of boats, yachts, and several venerable paddlewheel riverboats idled in the Mississippi.

Very few of those watching were aware of the tense drama that was being played at the top of the arch. The tips of the legs were only thirty inches from joining—exactly according to plan. A spreader jack forced the legs backward another six feet to accept the final section. That was according to plan, too. When the final sandwich was slipped into place, the jack would be removed, and the combined thrust of the keystone piece against the legs would greatly add to the total strength of the arch.

But there was a sudden problem. And a serious one. The sun was rapidly heating the south leg of the arch and threatening to deflect it off center. There was clear danger that St. Louis would, after all, have twin leaning towers, just as the skeptics had predicted. The only solution was to cool the leg with as much water as the builders could possibly pump. Water pumps were turned to full volume. The engineers figured that at best this would give them only about forty-five min-

"Topping off" day, when the final pyramid of the 142 was lifted into place. The last piece was raised to the tune of martial music, steamboats whistling on the Mississippi below. If you look closely you can see the American flag fluttering from the final triangle section.

utes to get the last sandwich in place before the leg turned off center.

In a race against the sun, one of the creeper derricks lowered a cable and hooked onto the final sandwich. The derrick operator drew in on the cable hoist. The final wedge went up; the breeze was so stiff that the American flag mounted on it stood straight out.

A transcript of the radio messages between workers on the ground and those at the top gives some hint of the tension:

"Coming up with the main load . . ."

"180 feet . . . 200 feet . . . 300 . . . 400 . . . 500 . . ."

"Easy now, Bill. Keep coming up. I may stop you anytime. Hold it. Hold it right there!"

There were long moments of silence as the piece was fitted. Then, as the jack was removed and the two legs clanked against the keystone sandwich, the men who had built the Gateway Arch knew that they had won. If there was one sixty-fourth inch showing anywhere, nobody could find it. There was no cheering on the creeper derrick platforms. But suddenly the workers became aware of whistles hooting in the Mississippi, more than 600 feet below them.

"What's that all about?" radioed one of the workers.

"I don't know . . . steamboats, I guess . . . celebratin'."

BIBLIOGRAPHY

American Heritage, editors of. *Let Freedom Ring. The Story of Independence Hall.* New York: American Heritage Publishing Co., 1962.
Bannister, Turpin C. "The Genealogy of the Dome of the United States Capitol. A paper presented before the Society of Architectural Historians, Boston, Mass., Jan. 29, 1948." *Society of Architectural Historians Journal,* Vol. 7, Nos. 1-2, Jan.-June, 1948.
Borglum, Lincoln. *My Father's Mountain, Mt. Rushmore National Memorial and How It Was Carved.* Rapid City, S.D.: Fenwinn Press, 1965.
Brown, Allen. *Golden Gate, Biography of a Bridge.* Garden City, N.Y.: Doubleday & Co., 1965.
Brown, Glenn. *History of the United States Capitol.* Vols. 1-2. Washington, D.C.: U.S. Government Printing Office, 1896.
Building of the Arch. St. Louis: Jefferson National Expansion Memorial Association (Robert F. Arteaga, photographer), 1972.
"The Capitol: House of Stewart." *Time,* Feb. 3, 1965; p. 26.
"The Capitol: The Falling Front." *Time,* Aug. 19, 1966; p. 22.
The Capitol. A pictorial story of the Capitol in general and the House of Representatives in particular. Washington, D.C.: U.S. Government Printing Office, 1959.
Chapelle, Howard I. *The History of the American Sailing Navy.* New York: Bonanza Books, 1949.
Chassley, Sey. "Capital Sundial." *Collier's,* Vol. 128, Dec. 1, 1951; p. 30.
Chester, Michael. *Joseph Strauss, Builder of the Golden Gate Bridge.* New York: G. P. Putnam's Sons, 1965.
Dean, Robert J. *Living Granite, the Story of Borglum and the Mount Rushmore Memorial.* New York: The Viking Press, 1949.
Ditzel, Paul C. "How They Built . . . and Rebuilt the White House." *The American Legion Magazine,* Oct. 1969; p. 18.
———. "How They Built the Nation's Capitol in Washington." *The American Legion Magazine,* Aug. 1970; p. 24.
———. "How They 'Built' the Washington Monument." *The American Legion Magazine,* Feb. 1968; p. 24.
———. "The Story of Old Ironsides." *The American Legion Magazine,* June 1966; p. 18.
———. "The Story of the Liberty Bell Since 1751." *The American Legion Magazine,* Dec. 1968; p. 25.
Donovan, Frank. *The Tall Frigates.* New York: Dodd, Mead and Co., 1962.

"The Erection of the White House." *Columbia Historical Society Record*, Vol. 16, p. 120, 1913; Vol. 33-34, p. 306, 1931.

Fite, Gilbert C. *Mount Rushmore.* Norman, Okla.: University of Oklahoma Press, 1952.

Forester, C. S. *The Age of Fighting Sail.* Garden City, N.Y.: Doubleday & Co., 1956.

Frary, I. T. *They Built the Capitol.* Richmond, Va.: Garret and Massie, Inc., 1940.

Freidel, Frank and Aikman, Lonnelle. *George Washington, Man and Monument.* Washington, D.C.: Washington National Monument Association, with the Cooperation of the National Geographic Society, 1973.

Gallagher, H. Pierce. *Robert Mills, Architect of the Washington Monument.* New York: Columbia University Press, 1935.

Gates, William H. (Compiler). *Hoover Dam, Including the Story of the Turbulent Colorado River.* Los Angeles: Wetzel Publishing Company, Inc., 1932.

The Golden Gate Bridge. Bethlehem, Pa.: Bethlehem Steel Corporation, *circa* 1937.

"Golden Gate Bridge: No. 1 U.S. Wonder." *Los Angeles Times*, Feb. 2, 1975; pt. 9, p. 2.

Golden Gate Bridge Highway and Transportation District, San Francisco. *Golden Gate Bridge, circa* 1972.

Gschaedler, Andre. *True Light on the Statue of Liberty and Its Creator.* Narberth, Pa.: Livingston Publishing Co., 1966.

Hall-Quest, Olga W. *The Bell That Rang for Freedom.* New York: E. P. Dutton and Company, Inc., 1965.

Handlin, Oscar. *Statue of Liberty.* New York: Newsweek Book Division, 1971.

Hansen, Harry. *Old Ironsides. The Fighting Constitution.* New York: Random House, 1955.

Harris, Marian Sands. "James Hoban." *The American-Irish Historical Society Journal*, Vol. 29, 1931; p. 49.

Harvey, Frederick (Compiler). *History of the Washington National Monument and Washington National Monument Society.* Washington, D.C.: U.S. Government Printing Office, 1903.

Hazleton, George C., Jr. *The National Capitol, Its Architecture, Art and History.* New York: J. F. Taylor Co., 1907.

Hicks, Clifford B. "The Incredible Gateway Arch." *Popular Mechanics*, Dec. 1963; p. 86.

"Highest Arch in the U.S." *Science Digest*, Feb. 1966; p. 9.

Hollis, Ira N. *The Frigate Constitution. The Central Figure of the Navy Under Sail.* Boston: Houghton Mifflin Co., 1931.

Horgan, Thomas P. *Old Ironsides. The Story of USS Constitution.* Boston: Burdette & Company, Inc., 1963.
Hurd, Charles. *The White House, A Biography.* New York: Harper & Bros., 1940.
"The Illness of The Liberty Bell." *The Literary Digest,* March 13, 1915; p. 542.
Kimball, Fiske. "The Genesis of the White House." *Century Magazine,* Feb. 1918; p. 523.
Kleinsorge, Paul L. *The Boulder Canyon Project, Historical and Economic Aspects.* Palo Alto, Calif.: Stanford University Press, 1941.
Kreh, Bill. "Monument Oddities." *The American Mercury,* Vol. 79, Nov. 1954; p. 73.
Leeming, Joseph. *The White House in Picture and Story.* New York: G. W. Stewart, 1953.
Levine, Benjamin and Story, Isabelle F. *Statue of Liberty National Monument, Liberty Island, N.Y.* Washington D.C.: National Park Service, Historical Handbook, Series No. 11, 1952.
Lieber, Leslie. "Washington Never Slept Here." *This Week Magazine,* Sept. 18, 1951; p. 7.
———. "Who's the Lady on the Capitol Dome?" *This Week Magazine,* July 3, 1960; p. 12.
McConnell, Jane and Burt. *The White House. A History with Pictures.* New York: Thomas Y. Crowell Co., 1954.
Mensch, E. Cromwell. *The Golden Gate Bridge, A Technical Description in Ordinary Language.* San Francisco: E. Cromwell Mensch, 1935.
Mitchell, Helen and Wilson, W. N. *Ships That Made History.* New York: Whittlesey House, 1950.
"The Most Beautiful Structure" (Washington National Monument). *Senior Scholastic,* Vol. 76, Feb. 24, 1960; p. 44.
The National Capitol. Federal Writers Project, 1937.
"The New White House." *Munsey's,* Vol. 29, April 1903; p. 65.
"Old Supreme Court Chamber Restored." *Los Angeles Times* (Associated Press), May 23, 1975; pt. 1, p. 20.
Our Capitol. 87th Congress, 1st Session, Senate Document No. 50. Washington, D.C.: U.S. Government Printing Office, 1961.
Pearce, John N. (Curator). *The White House, An Historic Guide.* Washington, D.C.: White House Historical Association, 1962.
Peattie, Donald Culross. "The Perfect Memorial." *The Reader's Digest,* Vol. 46, Feb. 1945; p. 95.
"Planes, Boats, Expenses . . . President's Pay Is Many Things." *U.S. News & World Report,* Jan. 27, 1969, p. 32.

Price, Willadene. *Bartholdi and the Statue of Liberty.* Chicago: Rand McNally & Co., 1959.

———. *Gutzon Borglum, Artist and Patriot.* Chicago: Rand McNally & Co., 1961.

Remsberg, Charles. "St. Louis' Two-Legged Tower: Tallest U.S. Monument." *Popular Science,* April 1964; p. 91.

Rhodes, Lynwood Mark. "Gutzon Borglum and His Colossal Statuary." *The American Legion Magazine,* Vol. 96, No. 1, Jan. 1974; p. 8.

Richard, Dorothy E. *Old Ironsides, The Glorious Career of the USS Constitution.* Navy Relief Society. undated.

Roosevelt, Theodore. *The Naval War of 1812.* New York: G. P. Putnam's Sons, 1927.

Rosewater, Victor. *The Liberty Bell, Its History and Significance.* New York: Appleton Company, 1926.

Schott, Joseph L. "How They Built the Nation's Capital." *The American Legion Magazine,* Aug. 1965; p. 18.

Sculptures at Hoover Dam. Bureau of Reclamation, U.S. Department of the Interior. Washington, D.C.: U.S. Government Printing Office, 1968.

Shuster, Alvin (Editor). *New York Times Guide to the Nation's Capital.* Washington, D.C.: R. B. Luce, 1967.

Singleton, Esther. *The Story of the White House.* Vols. 1-2. New York: The McClure Co., 1907.

Snow, Elliott and Gosnell, H. Allen. *On The Decks of 'Old Ironsides.'* New York: The Macmillan Co., 1932.

The Story of Hoover Dam. Bureau of Reclamation, U.S. Department of the Interior. Washington, D.C.: U.S. Government Printing Office, 1971.

Sutton, Horace. "Tall Tales." *Saturday Review,* Vol. 49, Dec. 18, 1965; p. 44.

"That Remodeling Job at the White House." *The Reader's Digest,* Vol. 61, Sept. 1952; p. 117.

"To Keep the Capitol from Falling Down." *U.S. News & World Report,* Oct. 25, 1965; p. 12.

United States Frigate 'Constitution,' a brief account of her history, together with data for model builders. Bureau of Construction and Repair, U.S. Navy Department. Washington, D.C.: U.S. Government Printing Office, 1932.

"Visitors Again Board 'Old Ironsides,' Renovated for Bicentennial." *Los Angeles Times,* March 15, 1975; pt. 1, p. 11.

Walker, John and Katharine. *The Washington Guidebook.* New York: Dell Publishing Company, Inc., 1963.

Warren, Charles. "The Washington National Monument Society." *The National Geographic Magazine,* Vol. 91, June 1947; p. 739.

"Washington Monument." *Holiday Magazine,* Vol. 25, Feb. 1959; p. 109.

"Washington Row: New Front for Capitol." *U.S. News & World Report,* July 4, 1966; p. 9.

"We, the People, The Story of the United States Capitol, Its Past and Its Promise. Washington, D.C.: The United States Capitol Historical Society in cooperation with The National Geographical Society, 1974.

Westcott, Allan. *American Sea Power Since 1775.* Philadelphia: J. B. Lippincott Co., 1947.

The White House. Federal Writers Project, 1927.

"The White House. Lady Bird's Last Hurrah." *Time,* Nov. 29, 1968; p. 13.

The White House. National Park Service, U.S. Department of the Interior. Washington, D.C.: U.S. Government Printing Office, 1962.

The White House, An Historic Guide. Washington, D.C.: White House Historical Association with the cooperation of the National Geographic Society, 1973 (revised edition).

"White House: No Fit Place to Live?" *U.S. News & World Report,* May 24, 1965; p. 48.

Willets, Gilson. *Inside History of the White House.* New York: The Christian Herald (Bible House), 1908.

Wolff, Perry. *A Tour of the White House with Mrs. John F. Kennedy.* Garden City, N.Y.: Doubleday & Company, Inc., 1962.

INDEX

Abington, Mass., 74
Adams, Abigail, 25
Adams, John, 13, 15, 25, 26, 35, 44, 57
Alameda, Calif., 158, 163
Alarcón, Hernando de, 131
All-American Canal, Calif. (*See* Hoover Dam)
Allentown, Pa., 13, 20
American Iron & Steel Institute, 176
American Museum of Immigration (*See* Statue of Liberty)
American Society of Civil Engineers, 144
Anderson, Happy, 120
Anderson, Melford O., 7
Annapolis, Md., 83
Anthony, Susan B., 117, 121
Aquia quarries, Va., 24, 39, 42
Arlington Memorial Bridge, Va., 147
Arthur, Chester A., 27, 66
Astor, William Waldorf, 99
Atlanta, Ga., 18, 104
Atlantic City, N.J., 78

Babcock & Wilcox Company, 140, 141
Bainbridge, William, 81
Bainbridge Island, Wash., 85
Baltimore, Md., 24, 39, 45, 52, 55, 66, 74, 84, 97
Baltimore & Susquehanna Railroad, 55
Bank of America, 156

Barbary pirates, 69, 71, 74, 76, 77, 78
Barberton, O., 140, 141
Barker, Josiah, 82
Bartholdi, Frédéric-Auguste, 4, 88, 90, 92, 93, 95, 97, 99, 101, 103
Battle of Lexington (1775), 12
Bechtel, Nev., 141
Bechtel, W. A., Company, 135
Bedloe's Island, N.Y. (*See* Statue of Liberty)
Beecher, Laban S., 82
Bentley, Samuel, 74
Bethlehem Steel Corporation, 157, 158
Bicentennial Celebration, U.S. (1976), 21, 45, 46, 86, 182
Black Hills, S.D., 104, 105, 106, 107, 109, 113
Blackbeard Island, Ga., 74
Bladensburg, Md., 46
Blagden, George, 39, 44
Blythe Island, Ga., 74
Bogardus, James, 47
Borglum, John Gutzon de la Mothe, 2, 4, 5, 103, 104, 105, 106, 107, 108, 109, 111, 113, *114,* 115, 117
Borglum, Lincoln, 107, 111, 113, 124
Boston, Mass., 12, 20, 25, 28, 44, 74, 76, 77, 78, 81, 82, 85, *86,* 97
Boston Tea Party (1773), 12, 28
Boulder City, Nev. (*See* Hoover Dam)
Boulder Dam (*See* Hoover Dam)

Index / 191

Bracken, Nev., 133
Brooklyn, N.Y., 166
Brooklyn Bridge, N.Y., 165
Brumidi, Constantino, 48
Buffalo, N.Y., 66
Bulfinch, Charles, 44, 46
Bunker Hill, Mass., 20
Bunker Hill Monument, Mass., 54

Calamity Jane, 107
Calexico, Calif., 142
Capitol Building, Washington, D.C., 1, 3, 22-24, 26, 36, *37, 38*, 39, 40, *41*, 42, *43*, 44-46, *47*, 48, *49*, 50, 52, 55, 57, 68, 90, 95, 105
  acoustic problems, 42, 44
  Apotheosis of George Washington, 48
  arguments over, 38, 39, 42
  assassination attempt (1835), 45
  basement crypt for Washington's body, 44, 48
  burning by British (1814), 43, 44
  Civil War, use during, 48
  cornerstone laying (1793), 38
  design competition (1792), 36, 37, *38*
  dimensions and facilities, 39, 48, 50
  dome, 37, *41*, 46, *47*, 48, 50
  extensions, 45, 46, 48
  fallen arches, 42, 43
  as a flea market, 45
  gas explosion (1898), 45
  House of Representatives, 37, 40, 42, 44, 45, 48, 50
  Jefferson and builder Latrobe, 42
  Library of Congress, 45
  National Statuary Hall, 44
  "Oven," 40
  Pocahontas statue, 46, *49*
  rotunda, 37-39, 44-46, 48, 105
  Senate, 37, 39, 40, 45, 48, 50
  Statue of Freedom, 46, 48, *49*, 50
  Supreme Court, 40, 45, 46
  Washington and builder Hallet, 38, 39
Carson, Kit, 106
Cary, George, 52
Casey, Thomas Lincoln, 61
Centennial Celebration, U.S. (1876), 18, 90, 93, *102*
Charles, Robert, 9
Charleston, S.C., 18, 23, 54

Chicago, Ill., 18, 97, 124
Cincinnati, O., 66
Civil War, 30, 47, 48, 59, 83, 127
Claghorne, George, 74, 76
Clark, William, 106, 170
Clay, Henry, 52
Cleveland, Grover, 103
Cleveland, O., 97
Coachella Valley, Calif., 127, 142, 143
Cody, "Buffalo Bill," 106
Colorado River, 125, *126*, 127, *128*, 129, *130*, 131, 132, 133, *134*, 135, *137*, 139, 142
Columbia Broadcasting Building, N.Y., 172
Conoly's Quarry, Md., 45
Constitution, U.S.S. (*See Old Ironsides*)
Coolidge, Calvin, 22, 28, 29, 32, 109, 111
Cordwainers, Boston, Mass., 76
Crawford, Thomas, 46
Crocker, Charles, 146
Crowe, Patrick J., 136
Custis, George Washington Parke, 55, 57

Dacres, James R., 78, 80
Davis, Jefferson, 45, 46
Dean, Robert J., 115
Declaration of Independence (1776), 7, 13, *14*, 15, 20, 54, 57, 106
Denver, Col., 135
Dewey, Samuel Worthington, 82
Diamond, James, *23*
Dickman, Bernard F., 170
Doughty, William, 71
Duke of Leinster, 23
Dulles International Airport, near Washington, D.C., 172

Eastman, S. P., 155
Edison, Thomas Alva, 99
Eiffel, Gustave, 92, 93, 94, 98, 101
Elliott, Jesse D., 82, 83
Empire State Building, N.Y., 143

Ford, Betty, 22
Ford, Gerald, 1, 22, 28
Fox, Josiah, 71
Franklin Institute, Philadelphia, Pa., 16, 20, 21

Frémont, John, 145
French, Benjamin B., 57

Garfield, James, 30
Gateway Arch (Jefferson National Expansion Memorial), St. Louis, Mo., 2, 4, 5, 6, 63, 170, *171*, 172, *173*, 174, *175*, 176, 177, *178*, 179, *180*, 181, 182, *183*, 184
  closed-circuit television, 178
  computer, use of, 5, 179
  concrete pouring, 176, 177, 179
  construction materials, 176
  cost, 173, 174
  creeper derricks, *173*, 175, 177, *178*, 179, 181, *183*, 184
  dangers, 170, 174, 175
  design competition (1947), 172, 173, 174
  final section placed (1965), 182, *183*
  foundations, 175, 176
  funding, 172
  gamma-radiation cameras, 5, 170, 177
  Jefferson National Expansion Memorial Association (1935), 172
  margin of error, 174, 178, 179
  Museum of Westward Expansion, 182
  nighttime measurements, 178, 179
  observation room, 182
  passenger trains, 182
  peak work force (1963-1964), 179
  race against the sun (1965), 182, *183*, 184
  safety net, *180*, 181
  size, 173, 174
  skepticism, 174
  spreader jack, 182
  stabilizing strut, *178*, *180*, 181
  stairway, 182
  steel sandwiches, 174, *175*, 176, 178, 179, *180*, 182, *183*
  swaying, 174, 177, 179, 181
  two-way radios, 178, 183, 184
  visitors center, 173, 175
  wind problems, 179, 181
  window sections, 181, 182
  X-raying, 176, 177
Giannini, A. P., 156

Gibbs, James, 24
Gila River, 128
Glendale, Calif., 131
Glover Island, Ga., 74
Golden Gate, Calif., 2, 145, *146*, 147, 148, 149, 150, 152, 154, *156*, 158, 159, *160*, 161, *162*, 163, 168, 169
Golden Gate Bridge, San Francisco, Calif., 2, 4, 6, 145, *146*, 147, *148*, 149, 150, *151*, 152, *153*, 154, 155, *156*, 157-159, *160*, 161, *162*, 163, *164*, *165*, 166, *167*, 168, 169
  anchorages and pylons, *156*, 157, 158
  arguments for, 149, 150, 155
  breathing allowance, 152, 154
  cable-spinning, *162*, 164, 165, 166
  caisson lost (1934), 161
  catwalks, *164*
  cement mixing and pouring, 158
  color, 167
  construction materials, 168
  construction starts (1933), 157, 158
  contracts let (1932), 157
  creeper derricks, 159, 161, 163
  dangers, 148
  deep-sea divers, 154, 155, 159, 161, 162
  designs, 147, 152, 154
  dimensions, 152
  dynamite bombs, 159, 161
  elephant trunks, 158
  fatal accidents (1936-1937), 166, 167, 168
  final rivet (1937), 168
  foghorns, 150
  funding, 149, 154, 156, 169
  Golden Gate Association, 149
  Golden Gate Bridge and Highway District Act of 1923, 149
  Golden Gate Ferries, Inc., 150, 155
  Great Depression (1929), 154, 157
  Half Way To Hell Club, 6, 165, 166
  Marin (Lime Point) pier and tower, *151*, 152, *153*, 154, *156*, 157, 158, *160*, 161, 162, 163, *164*, *167*
  memorial plaque, 168
  mermaid caverns, 154, 155
  myth of the buried locomotive, 167
  opening celebrations (1937), 168
  opposition to, 147, 148, 149, 150, 154, 155

riveting, 163, 168
roadway, *148,* 152, 157, *165,* 167, 168
rotary cement trucks, 158, 161, 162
safety net and other precautions, 149, *165,* 166, 168
San Francisco pier and tower, 150, *151,* 152, *153,* 154, 155, *156,* 157, 159, *160,* 161, *162,* 163, *164, 167*
ship crashes into bridge trestle (1937), 159
sidewalks, *148,* 152, 167, 168
storm and high sea damage (1933), 160, 161
suicides, 168
suspender ropes, *148*
suspension cables, *148, 156,* 157, *160, 162,* 163, 164, *165,* 166
swaying, 154, 164
traffic capacity, 168
Grand Canyon, 127
Grand Coulee Dam, Wash., 141
Grant, Ulysses S., 27, 28, 61, 99
Great Depression (*See* Golden Gate Bridge; Hoover Dam; Mount Rushmore)

Hadfield, George, 39
Half Way To Hell Club (*See* Golden Gate Bridge)
Hallet, Stephen, 36, 37, 38, 39
Hanover, Mass., 76
Hapgood, M. P., *53,* 61
Harrison, Benjamin, 27
Hart, Philip, 162
Hart, William S., 121
Hartt, Edmund, 74
Hartt, Edward, 74
Hartt, Joseph, 74
Hayes, Rutherford B., 62
Henry, Patrick, 36
Hepburn, David, 57
Hickok, Wild Bill, 107
Hoban, James, 5, 23, 24, 25, 26, 31, 32, 34, 35, 38, 39
Holmes, Oliver Wendell, 3, 81, 82, 85
Hoover, Herbert, 3, *29,* 129, 131, 135
Hoover Compromise, 129
Hoover Dam, 2, 5, 125, *126,* 127, *128,* 129-133, *134,* 135, *137,* 138, *139,* 140-142, *143,* 144
Black Canyon, 129, 132, 133, 135, 136, 137, 138, 141
Boulder Canyon Project Act of 1928, 130, 131
Boulder City, Nev., 135, 136
Boulder Dam, 131, 142
cement pouring, 139, 140, 141, 143
cofferdams, 138, 139
Colorado River Compact of 1922, 129, 130
construction appropriations, 130
construction equipment, 136
construction materials, 133, 140, 143
dedication (1935), 142
diversion tunnels, *137,* 138, 139, 142
dynamiting, 136, 137, 138, 139
first power contracts (1930), 131
first power generated (1936), *130,* 142, 143
Great Depression (1929), 131, 135, 136
high-scalers, 136
intake towers, *139,* 140, 141, 142
Lake Mead, *126,* 143, 144
name changes, 131
opposition to, 131, 132
outlet works, *139*
peak labor force (1934), 141
penstocks, *139,* 140
power-generating capacity, 141
powerplant, *130, 134,* 141
race against the Colorado River, 132, 136
Red Bull, 125, 129, 136, 142
reservoir, 127, 129, 132, 142, 143
significance of, 143, 144
site criteria, 127
Six Companies, Inc. (Big Six), 3, 135, 136, 137, 142
spillways, 138, *139,* 142
transmission towers and lines, 141
turbines, 141, 143
United States Construction Railroad, 133, 141
X-raying, 141
Hughes, Albert A., 18
Hughson, William L., 155
Hull, Isaac, 78, 82
Humphreys, Joshua, 71, 74
Hunt, Richard M., 95

194 / Index

Ickes, Harold L., 131
Imperial, Calif., 142
Imperial Valley, Calif., 125, 127, 132, 133, 142, 143, 144
Independence Hall, Philadelphia, Pa., 3, 8, *17*, 18, *19*, 21, 87 (*See also* State House, Philadelphia, Pa.)
Insull, Samuel, 111

Jackson, Andrew, 45, 54, 82, 83
Jefferson, Thomas, 1, 4, 15, 22, 23, 26, 36, 38, 39, 40, 42, 46, 54, 106, *112*, 113, 117-121, *122*, *124*, 170
Jefferson National Expansion Memorial, St. Louis, Mo. (*See* Gateway Arch)
Jordan, Wilfred, 16

Kaiser, Henry J., 136
Kennebec Valley, Me., 74
Kennedy, Jacqueline, 22, 27
Keystone, S.D., 108, 109, 117
Know Nothings (*See* Washington National Monument)
Knox, Henry, 71, 74, 76
Kolkmeier, Ken, 176, 177

Laboulaye, Édouard de, 88, 90, 95
Lafayette, Marquis de, 38
Lake Mead (*See* Hoover Dam)
Las Vegas, Nev., 129, 133
Latrobe, Benjamin Henry, 26, 40, 42, 43, 44
Lazarus, Emma, 97
Leaning Tower of Pisa, 174
Lee, Mass., 45
Leech, Thomas, 8
Leete's Island, Conn., 95
L'Enfant, Pierre Charles, 24, 36, 51, 55
Lenthal, John, 5, 40, 42, 43
Lewis, Meriwether, 106, 170
Liberty Bell, Philadelphia, Pa., 2, 3, 5, 7, *8*, *9*, 10, *11*, 12, 13, *14*, 15, 16, *17*, 18, *19*, 20, 21
  burial in Bethlehem, Pa. (1777), 15
  cracks, 10, 13, 16, 20
  distemper, 16, 18
  dynamite plot (1965), 21
  inscription, 9, 12

malignancy of the molecules, 16
naming, 13
noise pollution, 12
Philadelphians sue, 20
recastings (1752), 10, 11, 12
repairs, 18, 20, 21
ringing of, 12, 13, 15, 18
saved from the British (1777), *9*, 13, 14
saved from junking (1828), 15, 16
size, 11, 12
travels of, 11, 18, 20
wobbles, 20
Liberty Enlightening the World (*See* Statue of Liberty, N.Y.)
Liberty Island, N.Y. (*See* Statue of Liberty, N.Y.)
Lincoln, Abraham, 1, 27, 30, 47, 48, 57, 59, 88, 105, 106, *112*, 113, 118, 119, 120, 121, *123*, 124
Lincoln, Mary Todd, 27
Lord, John A., 85
Los Angeles, Calif., 131, 133, 141, 143, 144
Los Angeles Department of Water and Power, 131, 141
Louisiana Purchase Treaty (1803), 170, 172
Lower Boulder Canyon (*See* Hoover Dam, Black Canyon)

McClintic-Marshall Corporation, 157, 158
MacDonald & Kahn Company, Ltd., 136
MacDonald Construction Company, 175, 176
McKim, Charles F., 28
McNair, Andrew, 13
Madison, Dolley, 55
Madison, James, 26, 55, 78
Marsh, George Perkins, 62
Marshall, John, 16, 51, 52
Martin, Tyrone G., 86
Mead, Elwood, 133
Mears & Stainback Foundry, 18
Meigs, Montgomery C., 45, 46
Metropolitan Water District of Southern California, 131, 144

Mills, Clark, foundry, 46
Mills, Robert, 52, 54, 56, 58, 59, 62
Minneapolis, Minn., 97
Monroe, James, 44
Moore, Kermit, 166, 167
Morgan, John Pierpont, 99
Morrison-Knudsen Company, 136
Morrow, Irving F., 154
Morton, Levi P., 99
Mount Rushmore National Memorial, S.D., 2, 4, 5, 103, 104, *105*, 106, 107, *108*, 109, *110*, 111, *112*, 113, *114*, 115, *116*, 117, *118*, 119-121, *122*, *123*, 124, 168
   accidents (1936), 120
   cost, 109
   crack in Jefferson's face, 118, 119
   dedications, 109, 111, 117, *118*, 120, 121
   faces, choice of, 117
   final dynamite blast (1941), 124
   floodlighting, 121, 122
   fund-raising, 105, 106, 109, 115, 117, 119
   Great Depression (1929), 117
   Hall of Records, 121
   naming, 107
   Jefferson's face, 106, *112*, 113, 117, 118, 119, 120, 121, *122*, 124
   Lincoln's face, 106, 113, *116*, *118*, 120, 121, *123*, 124
   opposition to, 106
   Roosevelt's face, 106, 115, 117, 121, *123*, 124
   size of faces, 109
   transferring studio model measurements, 111, 113, 115
   Washington's face, 106, 109, *110*, 111, 113, 115, 118, 119, *122*, 124
Mount Vernon, Va., 23, 25, 32, 44, 52

New Orleans, La., 18
New York, N.Y., 4, 47, 63, 66, 74, 84, 88, 90, 93, 97, 107, 140, 143, 163
Newport, R.I., 83
Niagara Falls Suspension Bridge, 165
Nicholson, Samuel, 74
Nixon, John, 13
Nixon, Richard, 22

Norbeck, Peter, 106, 109, 111, 115, 117, 120
Norfolk, Va., 74, 83, 84
Norris, Isaac, 8, 9, 10, 11
Northampton, Pa. (*See* Allentown, Pa.)
Norton I, Emperor of the United States and Protector of Mexico, 145, 147
Norton, Joshua A. (*See* Norton I)

Oakland, Calif., 161
Old Ironsides (U.S.S. *Constitution*), 3, 5, 69, *70*, 71, 72, 73, 74, 75, 76, 77, 78, 79, *80*, 81, 82, *83*, *84*, 85, *86*, 87
   annual turnaround cruise, 86
   armament, 72, 73
   battle with the *Cyane* and the *Levant* (1815), 81
   battle with the Guerrière (1812), 15, 78, *79*, 80, 81
   battle with the *Java* (1812), 81
   coins placed under the masts, 85
   cost, 76
   design, 71, 72, 73
   frigates, described, 69, 71
   Hercules figurehead, 76, 77, 78
   hunting slave ships (1852), 83
   Jackson figurehead decapitated (1834), 82, 83
   launching (1797), 76, 77
   naming of, 69, 73, 80
   poem by Oliver Wendell Holmes (1834), 81, 82
   proposed junking, 81, 85
   reconstruction, *83*, 85, 86
   size, 71, 72, 73
   speed, 73
   used as a barracks, *84*
   used as a school, 83
Old South Church, Boston, Mass., 28
Outerbridge, Alexander E., Jr., 16, 18, 20

Pacific Bridge Co., 136, 157, 159-162
Paine, Clifford E., 152
Parliamentary Acts of 1768, 12
Pasadena, Calif., 131
Pass, John, 2, 10, 11, 12, 18
Pensacola, Fla., 85
Philadelphia, Pa., 3, 4, 8, *9*, 10, 13, *14*, 16, 18, 20, 22, 25, 26, 37, 38, 39, 40,

196 / Index

66, 71, 74, 87, 90, 93, 97, 158
Pierce, Franklin, 27
Pittsburgh, Pa., 176
Pittsburgh-Des Moines Steel Company (PDM), 176, 177
Polk, James K., 27, 55
Portsmouth, N.H., 74
Pottstown, Pa., 158
Pritchard, Art, 175
Pulitzer, Joseph, 4, 95, 99, 101

Quakers, 8, 71

Ramee, Daniel, 54
Rapid City, S.D., 104, 106, 109
Reed, Philip, 46
Revere, Paul, 5, 76
Richardson, Friend W., 149
Richmond, Va., 24, 26, 39, 52
Robinson, Doane, 104, 106, 111, 121
Roebling, John A., 157, 164, 165
Roosevelt, Franklin D., 22, 30, 35, 119, 120, 131, 142, *143*, 172
Roosevelt, Theodore, 26, 28, 30, 106, 115, 117, 121, *123*, 124
Root, Erastus, 52
Rushmore, Charles E., 107

Saarinen, Eero, 172, 173
St. Louis, Mo., 18, 97, 170, *171*, 172, *173*, 174, *175*, 176, *178*, *180*, 182, *183*
Salton Sea, Calif., 125, 132
San Antonio, Tex., 107, 111
San Bernardino, Calif., 135
San Diego, Calif., 144
San Francisco, Calif., 20, 135, 136, 143, 145, *146*, 149, 154, 155, 156, 158, 159, 163, 165, 168
San Francisco-Oakland Bay Bridge, Calif., 158
Santa Fe Railway, 155
Sausalito, Calif., 147, 150
Seattle, Wash., 85
Sever, James, 77
Shea, J. F., Company, 136
Shoemaker, Ted, 107
Sioux Indians, 121
Six Companies, Inc. (*See* Hoover Dam)
Skillings Brothers, Boston, Mass., 76
Slattery, Charles, 87

Slaughterhouse Rock, S.D., 107
Slave labor, 5, 24, 39, 42
Smith, Luther Ely, 170
Smith, Moses, 80
Smithsonian Institution, Washington, D.C., 22, 27
Southern California Edison Company, 131
Southern Pacific Railroad, 146, 150, 155
Stamp Act of 1765, 12
Stanford, Leland, 146
Stanley, Edwin, 168
State House, Philadelphia, Pa., 7, 8, 10, 12, 13, *14*, 15 (*See also* Independence Hall)
Staten Island, N.Y., 97, 166
Statue of Freedom (*See* Capitol Building, Washington, D.C.)
Statue of Liberty, Liberty Island, N.Y., 4, 18, 62, 88, *89*, 90, *91*, *92*, 93, *94*, 95, *96*, 97, *98*, 99, *100*, 101, *102*, 103, 104, 168, 173
  American Committee on the Statue of Liberty, 95
  American Museum of Immigration, 103
  artists' criticism, 97
  Bartholdi's conception, 90
  Bedloe's Island, N.Y., 88, 90, 93, 95, 97, 99, 101, 103
  coins placed in pedestal (1886), 101
  color, choice of, 103
  copper, choice of, 90
  cost, 90
  dedication (1886), 103
  dimensions, 93, 103
  dynamite plot (1965), 21
  first elevator (1909), 103
  framework, 93, *94*, *96*, 101
  Franco-American Union, 90, 95, 97
  fund-raising, 90, 93, 95, 97, 99, 101
  Gaget, Gauthier & Cie, 90, 93, *98*, 99
  "Give me your tired, your poor . . . ," 97
  Liberty Enlightening the World, 90, 97
  Liberty Island, N.Y., 103
  opposition to, 97
  packing and shipping, 99, 101
  pedestal, 90, 93, 95, 101
  poem "The New Colossus," 97

presentation to the U.S. (1884), 99
reassembling (1886), 101, 103
rivets, number of, 101
torch, *89*, 90, 103
transforming statuette into full-sized statue, 90, 91, 92
Steelton, Pa., 158
Stewart, J. George, 50
Stone, Charles P., 95, 99, 101
Stone Mountain Confederate Memorial, Ga., 104, 105, 106, 107, 109, 111, 113
Stow, John, Jr., 2, 10, 11, 12, 18
Strauss, Joseph Baermann, 2, 147, 148, 149, 150, 152, 154, 161, 164, 166, 167, 168, 169
Student contributions, 3, 22, 58, 66, 85, 99, 109
Symington, Thomas, 55

Tennessee Valley Authority, 131
Thornton, William, 36, 37, 38, 39, 40, 42, 50
Tigris River, 125
Trans World Airlines terminal, N.Y., 172
Trenton, N.J., 51, 165
Truman, Harry, 22, 30, 31, 32, 34
Tucker, Jesse G., 109, 111

Union Pacific Railroad, 133
U.S. Bicentennial Celebration (*See* Bicentennial Celebration, U.S.)
U.S. Centennial Celebration (*See* Centennial Celebration, U.S.)
U.S. Bureau of Reclamation, Dept. of the Interior, 3, 127, 128, 132, 133, 135, 140, 142, 143
U.S. Coast and Geodetic Survey, 147
U.S. Corps of Engineers, 61, 62, 63
U.S. Dept. of the Interior, 172
U.S. Geological Survey, 128
U.S. Park Service, Dept. of the Interior, 68, 103, 119, 144
Unity, Me., 74
Utah Construction Company, 136

Verrazano-Narrows Bridge, N.Y., 166

Walter, Thomas U., 45, 95
War of 1812, 26, 29, 43, 73, 78, *79*, 80, 81, 90
Warner, Edward, 8
Washington, D.C., 24, 48, 68, 90, 95, 147, 172, 176
Washington, George, 1, 13, 15, 22-26, 36, 38, 39, 44, 51-68, 71, 106, 109, *110*, 111, 113, 115, 117-119, *122*, 124
Washington, John Augustine, 52
Washington, Martha, 26, 44, 52, 55
Washington National Monument, Washington, D.C., 3, 51, 52, *53*, 54, 55, *56*, 57-59, *60*, 61-63, *64*, *65*, 66, *67*, 68, 90, 104, 143, 173
  alignment problems, 62
  annual checkup, 62
  annual fireworks display, 66
  architectural sketches, *53*, 54, 61, 62
  capstone placed (1884), 63, *64*, *65*
  Civil War, use during, 59
  construction starts (1848), 57
  cornerstone laying (1848), 55, 57
  cost, 66
  decorative stones, 58, 66
  dedication (1885), 66
  dimensions, 66
  dynamite plot (1965), 21
  elevator, 66
  fund-raising, 54, 55, 59, 61
  hauling marble slabs, *60*
  height, 62
  Know Nothings, 58, 59, 62
  life net rigged, 63
  moisture problems, 68
  opened to the public (1888), 66
  opposition to, 59
  peepholes, 62
  pigeon, use of to fly wire, 61
  placing of coins (1880), 62
  Pope's stone, 58
  settling, 62
  steps and stairs, 66
  stunts, 66, 68
  sundial, 68
  swaying, 66
  unsafe foundations, 61, 62
  visitors, 68
Washington National Monument Society, 52, 54, 58, 59, 61, 62
Washington's Ring, 63
weight, 66

Watterson, George, 52
Webster, Daniel, 57
Weehawken, N.J., 97
West Coast Lumbermen's Association, 85
White House, Washington, D.C., 1, 3, 5, 22, *23*, 24-28, *29*, 30, *31*, 32, *33*, 34-36, 38, 39, 42, 44, 51, 68
  bomb shelter, 30, 34
  during Civil War, 30
  cockroach infestation, 27
  cornerstone laying (1792), 24
  cutting corners to save money, 25
  design competition (1792), 22, 23
  East Room, 25, 30, 31
  facilities, 25, 34, 35
  fires, 3, 26, *29*, 32
  firetrap, 28
  first elevator (1881), 27
  first gas lights (1848), 27
  first hot water system (1852), 27
  first occupants (1800), 25
  furniture auction (1881), 27
  laundry room, 25
  Lincoln Room, 27, 34
  mantel prayer, 35
  mysterious noises, 28, 30, 31
  naming of, 26
  Presidents' children, 30
  rat extermination, 28
  reconstructions, 26, 28, 31, 32, 34
  roof raised by Coolidge, 28, 29, 32
  sagging floors and ceilings, 27, 28, 31
  size, 34, 35
  souvenirs of, 32
  swaying chandelier, 30
  Truman Balcony, 1, 30, *33*
  Truman's sinking bathtub, 30
Whitechapel Foundry, London, England, 9, 10, 18
Wilbank, John, 15, 16
Wilbur, Ray Lyman, 132, 133
Wilkins, James H., 146, 147
Williamson, William, 106
Wilson, Woodrow, 117
Winthrop, Robert C., 57

Yuma, Ariz., 132, 142, 143
Yuma Valley, Ariz., 128, 129, 143